MW00330084

For Fred,
to whom Staten Island
was a foreign country.

BLUE GUIDE

STATEN ISLAND

A BLUE GUIDE TRAVEL MONOGRAPH

Carol V. Wright

Somerset Books • London

CONTENTS

Introduction

A Staten Island of the Mind
7

Robert Moses and Staten
Island 11

The Lay of the Land

Geology 14

Geography 17

Staten Island's islands 20

**Some Staten Island
Neighborhoods** 23

The North Shore 24

The West Shore 36

The East Shore 39

The Midline 44

The South Shore 48

Maritime Staten Island

The Staten Island Ferry 54

Sailors' Snug Harbor 61

John A. Noble, Salvage
Artist 70

The Oysters of Staten Island
74

Sandy Ground 78

The Lighthouses of Staten
Island 85

Frank Lloyd Wright on
Staten Island 92

Natural Staten Island 94

Staten Island Naturalists 95

Henry David Thoreau on
Staten Island 103

Frederick Law Olmsted
on Staten Island 105

The Greenbelt 110

Fresh Kills 116

Freshkills Park 120

Women of Staten Island

Alice Austen 126

Jacques Marchais and the
Museum of Tibetan Art 134

Staten Island Saints 140

3 4873 00490 6533

The Vanderbilts on Staten Island 141

The Vanderbilt Mausoleum 144

The Staten Island Bluebelt 147

The Bridges of Richmond County

The New Jersey Bridges 148

The Verrazano-Narrows Bridge 152

Military Staten Island

The Struggle for Settlement 157

The Revolutionary War 162

The Civil War 167

Fort Wadsworth 169

World War II: Miller Field 174

Ethnic Staten Island

The Ethnic Mix 176

The Victory Diner 178

Italian Staten Island 179

Garibaldi and Meucci 180

Our Lady of Mt Carmel 184

Gangsters and Guidos 187

The Outcasts of the Island

Staten Island as Refuge 191

The Quarantine 192

New York City Farm Colony 194

Seaview Hospital 201

Willowbrook 206

Practical Information

When You Visit: Contact Listings 209

Transportation 220

Hotels 222

Restaurants 222

Further Reading 226

Timeline 231

Maps

Overview 6

Detail 260–63

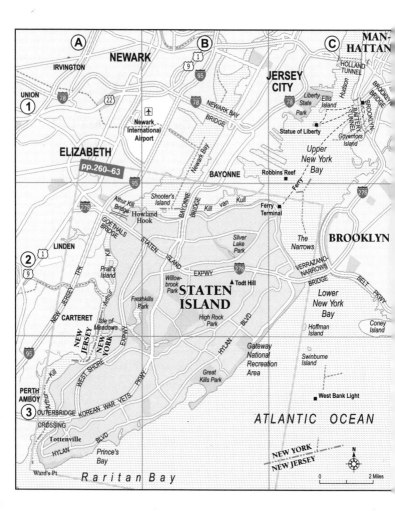

INTRODUCTION:
A STATEN ISLAND OF THE MIND

New York City is an archipelago, a collection of islands large and small surfacing through the Hudson and East Rivers, Upper and Lower New York Bays, Long Island Sound, Jamaica Bay, and the Atlantic Ocean. With the exception of the Bronx, which is appended to mainland North America, each the city's five boroughs is an island in itself, and Staten Island is the most "islandic" of all. Its geographical isolation has shaped its history more profoundly than insularity has affected the other boroughs. For many years accessible from the rest of New York only by boat (though linked to industrial New Jersey by three vehicular bridges and a railroad bridge), Staten Island has developed its own culture, its own politics, its own landscape, its own lore. The ties joining it to its fellow boroughs are more fragile than those that have bound the rest of the city together as Greater New York since 1898.

Staten Island's image in the minds of many people—a large number of whom have never been there—is unfortunate. Mention New York City to outsiders and you're likely to evoke thoughts of money, power, glitter, glamour, and so on. Mention Staten Island to an off-islander and you may well elicit a smirk, a snicker, or even a Bronx cheer. Labeled the "woebegone borough," the "orphaned borough," the "forgotten fifth," even compared to a retarded distant cousin, it is the butt of unkind jokes, beginning with one about the origin of the name: Henry Hudson, anchoring in the Narrows, pointed to a landmass off the port bow and asked his mate, "Iss dat an eyelandt?" (Why the English explorer should have spoken with a thick pseudo-Dutch accent remains unclear.) Some see Hudson's "eyelandt" as a way station on the road to somewhere else—an idea that seems to have taken root in the mind of urban planner Robert Moses, who rammed expressways through it so that travelers could get from Long Island to New Jersey without stopping at a single red light (*for more on Moses, see p. 11*). Other people have seen it as a place to consign anything unwanted, dreaded, or feared: the Island has harbored New York City's poor, its mentally ill, its actual or possible carriers of disease, as well as orphans, derelict ships, and, monumentally, the city's garbage—tons and tons and tons of it.

Of late the media has had a field day with the Island's image, notably on a couple of TV "reality" shows: *Mob Wives*, a "docu-soap," details the travails of four tough women making do while their convicted husbands are doing time; and *Jersey Shore* featured several Staten Islanders cast in stereotypically Italian-American roles. Mayor Michael Bloomberg, who should have known better, gave the Island the back of his hand when, newly in office, he suggested that the hostile press corps be banished there, to New York City's equivalent of Siberia. Even the freebie tabloid *Metro* couldn't resist a jab: when New York health commissioners rated the Island's restaurants the city's cleanest, *Metro's* front-page headline read, "Cleanest Dining on Staten Island" but the subhead snickered: "City dump has the cleanest kitchens?" (Later the paper edited the web site, softening the line.)

The image doesn't entirely conform to reality: it's an attitude, a projected Staten Island of the Mind. Outsiders may scoff, but Staten Islanders speak fondly, if defensively, of their home. It is the borough of parks. It has, even now, beautiful scenery. It is affordable, though increasingly less so. Its neighborhoods are neighborly. It has long inspired local loyalty, expressed in more than a century of committed volunteerism for urban planning, ecology, and historic preservation. The borough has its own daily newspaper, *Staten Island Advance*, founded in 1886, which proudly reports local news in a quirky hometown style: high school sports, prom fashions, local crime ("Teen robs Staten Island seniors, then asks, 'Where can I get a cab?' "), and local achievements ("PS 22 chorus will sing at 2013 presidential inaugural"). From time to time the paper's web site lists as a category "Weird Staten Island News" ("Homeowner awakens to snake slithering in toilet bowl").

Staten Island *is* different from the rest of the city. Physically, it's isolated, the only borough with no direct vehicular connection to Manhattan and no subway. It is the smallest in population (a little more than 470,000, compared to Brooklyn's 2,532,645) and the whitest (64 percent, down from 76 percent in 2000, and from 80 percent in 1990), with a large proportion of second- and third-generation Italian Americans. Economically, the borough is solidly middle class. The median household income in 2010 was $70,560, compared with $55,603 for the city at large. Staten Island has the city's highest proportion of government workers (fire fighters, police officers, teachers, sanitation workers, clerical workers), 22 percent in 2010. Its poverty rate is also lower than that of the city at large, with ten percent of the population below the poverty line, as opposed to 14 percent for the city as a whole.

It is the most suburban borough, its housing stock largely single-family or semi-detached houses rather than high-rise apartments. Perhaps because of its prosperity, the borough is politically conservative, voting Republican, while the other boroughs remain bastions of Democratic loyalty.

Staten Islanders do have legitimate gripes stemming either from governmental neglect or meddling. Potholes riddle the borough's streets, weeds and vines flourish in the parks, traffic crawls along during rush hours, public transportation is cumbersome, and bridge tolls are exorbitant. In a 1993 referendum, 65 percent of the population voted to secede from the City of New York, and while the split was averted by court action and the redress of some grievances, sentiment for secession was again rising a decade later. In the past twenty years, Staten Island has changed more than any other borough. It has become more ethnically and racially mixed, better educated, wealthier (but more expensive). The challenges remain: infrastructure, transportation, traffic control, and suburban sprawl all need to be addressed.

And while many things in the borough have changed or are changing, its image, the Staten Island of the Mind, remains stubbornly the same.

Robert Moses and Staten Island

Robert Moses (1888–1981) changed the physical face of New York City more than any other single person. His reign began in 1934 when Fiorello La Guardia appointed him the City's first commissioner of parks, making him lord of an empire embracing all five boroughs. Moses quickly accreted power, at his peak holding twelve public offices (none of them elective) at state and city levels. Directly or indirectly he controlled roads, urban renewal, housing, bridges, parks, and two World's Fairs; he influenced landfill, sanitation, and zoning policies. He brilliantly found or created sources of funding that protected him from the entanglements of local and state politics. He was a skillful drafter of legislation, a master of publicity, a paragon of preparedness, an ogre for work, a dictator, and a manipulator.

As long as his vision coincided with that of the world around him, he maintained his power. The press and the public admired him during the 1940s for his efforts at modernizing the City's antiquated housing and road infrastructures, but opposition arose in the 1950s. His mega-highways slashed through settled (usually poor or working-class) neighborhoods, destroying their social and economic fabric; the environmental consequences of his love affair with the automobile gradually became evident; and his arrogance and high-handedness galvanized powerful enemies who itched to strip him of his power. Robert Caro's Pulitzer-Prize-winning biography, *The Power Broker* (1974), expresses eloquently and vehemently the changed attitudes that brought about the decline of Moses' reputation: the recognition that bigger isn't always better, that public transportation has a place in urban planning, that neighborhood life is worth nurturing, and that open space left in its natural state has value independent of architecturally designed parks.

Staten Island, like the other boroughs, has paid the price of Moses' priorities. The lingering presence of the Fresh Kills Landfill (*see p. 116*) and the unbridled suburbanization that followed the Verrazano-Narrows Bridge are part of his legacy, as is the gridlock on its major roads. As early as the 1930s, Moses vigorously campaigned for a system of highways that would link Montauk on the eastern tip of Long Island with New Jersey, absorbing Staten Island into the regional highway network. His landscaped expressways would reach from bridge to bridge, carving up interior Staten Island and girdling its shoreline. Only parts of his plan were completed. The rest remains as half-built stubs, highways to nowhere, expressways that funnel into local streets. In the meantime, Staten Island's train and bus service has suffered.

Since the 1980s, however, Moses' reputation has been ascending again. As bureaucracy has made government increasingly inert, observers have recognized his phenomenal success in getting things done, his high design standards, and the fact that his improvements to infrastructure have made the city more livable in many ways. In all fairness, Moses pushed for the Bridge, but he also foresaw the rapid growth of Staten Island's post-bridge population and urged zoning to inhibit the construction of thousands of little houses huddled wall to wall on cramped lots; he also advocated the expenditure of City money to preserve open land. As the population of Staten Island burgeons, its traffic jams thicken, and its open space dwindles, the question of environmental values continues to pose difficult choices.

THE LAY OF THE LAND

"The history of any region is controlled to a large extent by its topography and that in turn is determined by its geology. Wherefor[e] it seems logical to begin the history of Staten Island with an account of its natural features..."

So begins *Staten Island and Its People*, the landmark history, written in 1930 by Charles W. Leng and William T. Davis, two early-twentieth-century historians who were also enthusiasts of science.

THE GEOLOGY OF STATEN ISLAND

"Fifty thousand years ago, Staten Island lay under the Wisconsin Glacier, a massive ice sheet perhaps a thousand feet thick in New York (but five times that deep in the Adirondacks and ten times that deep in Labrador), whose last forward creep halted about 22,000 years ago. This ice sheet, the largest and most recent of four that overspread much of the North American continent during the Pleistocene epoch, shaped much of Staten Island's terrain as we know it today. Plowing slowly southward, perhaps a foot a day, the glacier scraped up loose material in its path, gouging the underlying bedrock and dragging along boulders, rocks, gravel, and sand. This debris sculpted the bedrock beneath, sometimes scoring it with deep grooves, sometimes polishing it.

Then as the climate warmed, the glacier began to recede, vacating what is now metropolitan New York 12–15,000 years ago, stranding the load of debris along its southern boundary like seaweed after a high tide. This stripe of glacial debris, the terminal moraine, stretches from Cape Cod in Massachusetts, across Long Island, through Jamaica Hills, Crown Heights, and Bay Ridge in Queens and Brooklyn, across the Narrows, and through Staten Island (from the locale of the Verrazano-Narrows Bridge to Tottenville) before continuing westward.

As the ice sheet continued melting, retreating north and west, it deposited its load of unsorted boulders, rocks, gravel, and sand along its path. In Staten Island, this sediment, called glacial till, parallels the moraine to its west and accounts for the flattish landscape of such places as Travis and Bulls Head, areas that many centuries later would be cultivated for wheat and produce, or mined for clay and trap rock. It also accounts for the marshland of Fresh Kills that developed over the eons, as the higher moraine to the east shed most of its rainwater westward. The modifying effect of the Hudson estuary would eventually create a microclimate in which fertile ecosystems and plant communities would emerge, aided by the glacial soils and drainage patterns.

Meanwhile, as the glacier continued to recede, streams of water carrying suspended particles of gravel, sand, and silt flowed eastward toward the Atlantic from its melting edge. As these streams slowed, they deposited their cargo, eventually creating an outwash plain, with the coarsest particles near the moraine and the finer sand and silt forming a gentle slope further away. On Staten Island, east of the moraine, the flat, sandy outwash plain faces the Lower Bay, encompassing such low-lying present neighborhoods as New Dorp, South Beach, and Midland Beach.

The moraine, like a gigantic earthen dam, trapped behind it the melting waters of the glacier, which pooled into immense lakes, drowning the valleys gouged by the glacier and exerting pressure against the dam itself. Eventually the pressure became so great that the dam gave way near Staten Island, the fissure through what is now the Narrows. The dammed water poured outward, draining the lakes and deepening the Hudson channel beneath the Narrows, today one of the most important waterways on the eastern seaboard.

Staten Island serpentinite

Far older than the features chiseled out and piled up by the glacier is the bedrock of the Island's rocky spine of serpentine hills, which extends from St. George to Richmondtown. Here are Fort Hill, Pavilion Hill, Ward Hill, Grymes Hill, Emerson Hill, Ocean Terrace, and, highest of all, Todt Hill whose 409.24 feet make it the highest natural elevation on the eastern seaboard south of Maine.

Staten Island's serpentinite, some 35 square miles of bedrock underlying the central spine, dates back to the Paleozoic era, about 430 million years ago, when it originated deep within the prehistoric ocean at the boundaries of the tectonic plates. During the Paleozoic, the plate containing the prehistoric North American continent collided with the plate containing prehistoric Africa; a piece of ocean crust broke off and became incorporated into the collision zone. The remnant of this fragment has become Staten Island's oldest bedrock, serpentinite, a rare bluish gray mineral that contains large amounts of magnesium and iron, antigorite, chrysotile, and lizardite. It may feel slippery or soapy; it may be veined with fibrous chrysotile, a form of asbestos. Between 1858 and 1892 the H.W. Johns Company (later Johns Manville) mined Staten Island's serpentinite deposits, using the asbestos for fire-resistant shingles. Local architects, Ernest Flagg for one, used the stone for building

THE GEOGRAPHY OF STATEN ISLAND

Staten Island, since 1898 a borough of New York City, lies in Upper New York Bay, about five miles from the southern tip of Manhattan, a mile and a quarter from Brooklyn, and 672 feet from New Jersey if you count the over-water central span of the Goethals Bridge as the shortest distance. It is pear-shaped, occupies about 60 square miles, and has 35 miles of coastline. It is the third largest borough in size, but the smallest in population, though it is growing faster than any other borough, as is its foreign-born population.

The waterway on the north, the **Kill van Kull**, which runs between Upper New York Bay and Newark Bay in New Jersey, got its odd name—odd at least to English speakers—from the Dutch colonists who settled New Netherland in the seventeenth century and seeded the land with place names. In Middle Dutch, a *kille* was a stream, riverbed, or channel. The "kull" part is trickier. Early explorers usually named their discoveries either honorifically to flatter their patrons or descriptively to illustrate geographic or topological features. Some commentators assert that in Middle Dutch a *kol* is a ridge or a mountain pass and that the ridge in question is the rocky neck of land today called the Bayonne Peninsula. Thus the Kill van Kull is the "channel through the ridge," that is, the way to get to Newark Bay from New York Bay.

The Kill van Kull is three miles long and about a thousand feet wide, narrow and shallow enough to make navigation hazardous. The Robbins Reef Lighthouse in the Upper Bay signals the entrance to the Kill. The Bayonne Bridge spans it near its western end. Since colonial times, it has been a major commercial waterway, and nowadays enables container ships and oil tankers to reach Port Newark–Port Elizabeth, the nation's third largest container port. The Kill is shallow as well as narrow and has to be dredged, the most recent dredging deepening it to fifty feet. Along the Kill van Kull are the Island's older industrial communities, the water and solid upland making the area suitable for factories and shipping.

To the west, dividing the Island from New Jersey, the **Arthur Kill**, about ten miles long, connects Raritan Bay with Newark Bay. Like the Kill van Kull, it is being dredged to fifty feet to accommodate larger ships, a process that involves blasting the bedrock beneath the silt and layers of glacial material. On the New Jersey side, the infamous "Chemical Coast" wafts pollution eastward. On the Staten Island side are salt marshes, some of which have been filled and put to commercial or industrial uses, or planted with tract housing. Geologically, the Arthur Kill is thought to be the bed of a former channel for the Hudson River, whose course was altered by the terminal moraine damming up its present mouth through the Narrows.

Thus Staten Island's west coast parallels New Jersey, and geographically "belongs" to New Jersey; so it isn't surprising that for about 200 years New York and New Jersey bickered over the border along the Kill. In 1665, the Duke of York, by then proprietor of the former Dutch New Netherland, bestowed everything between the Hudson and the Delaware Rivers on a whim to two old friends, who called the place New Jersey and began making their own land grants. Unaware of York's decision Richard Nicolls, the deputy governor of New York, gave away the same land. New Jersey thus claimed political control of Staten Island based on the original land grant;

New York countered, claiming jurisdiction over Staten Island as far as the low water mark on the west side of the Arthur Kill. The dispute continued until 1833, when both states mutually agreed on the border, which today runs more or less through the middle of the Kill.

Staten Island's islands

Within Staten Island's official borders lie five small, uninhabited islands. Thanks to a throng of vocal environmentalists, all are protected as breeding grounds for wading birds: egrets, herons, ibises.

The three islands washed by the polluted tides of the kills—**Isle of Meadows**, **Prall's Island**, and **Shooter's Island**—are mostly salt marsh with some upland meadow. The Dutch farmed them for salt hay, but in later centuries the looming presence of New Jersey's "Chemical Coast" and the escalating marine traffic led to more destructive uses. Muck dredged from the Arthur Kill to keep it navigable for ever larger vessels was dumped on Isle of Meadows at the mouth of Fresh Kills, and as the hills of the infamous Fresh Kills dump (*see p. 116*) rose higher, Isle of Meadows only narrowly escaped becoming part of that festering heap. In the 1970s someone thought Prall's Island, further up the Arthur Kill, ideal for a bus depot, but fortunately the notion remained only a bizarre pipe dream. Shooter's Island, at the confluence of the Kill van Kull and the Arthur Kill, was a hunting preserve and a rendezvous for Revolutionary War spies before being given over to farming, petroleum refining and, finally, shipbuilding. Today the rotting pilings of former piers and the wooden dry dock walls remain from its glory days when the firm of Townsend & Downey turned out racing and cruising yachts, including the *Meteor*, built for Kaiser Wilhelm II and christened by Alice Roosevelt in 1902. Shooter's Island was abandoned around 1921 and for several decades was one of New York harbor's five ship graveyards. (New Jersey owns about one-third of Shooter's Island.)

The two islands in the Lower Bay, **Swinburne and Hoffman Islands**, both artificially created by landfill, came into being to accommodate the quarantine station, formerly in Tompkinsville, which Staten Islanders had burned to the ground. The quarantine facility opened on Hoffman Island in 1873, detaining all passengers arriving in the port with visible symptoms of illness; it remained open until 1927. Before World War II, a US Maritime Training Service station operated here, converting a building formerly used for delousing immigrants into a boat shed. Smaller Swinburne Island hosted a hospital and a crematorium. During World War II, both islands served as anchorages for underwater nets stretching across the mouth of the harbor to entangle submarines. Like the other harbor islands, these two attracted assorted development proposals: Mayor Fiorello La Guardia wanted a camp for poor children; urban planner Robert Moses wanted a park linked to Staten Island by landfill;

Staten Island borough president Joseph Palma wanted a dog track or an amusement park; and Staten Islanders themselves wanted homeless shelters, built here instead of in their home neighborhoods. Today, inhabited by herons, egrets, cormorants, and gulls, and visited sometimes by harbor seals, the islands are part of Gateway National Recreation Area.

GATEWAY NATIONAL RECREATION AREA

Gateway National Recreation Area, added to the national park system in 1972, preserves and makes publicly available—remarkably so in a densely populated urban area—some of New York Harbor's resources. Its 26,000 acres of coastal and underwater lands, which reach from Jamaica Bay in Queens to Sandy Hook in New Jersey, draw 11 million visitors annually to enjoy swimming, cycling, hiking, camping, fishing, and bird watching. The Staten Island units of Gateway are Great Kills Park, much of Miller Field, Hoffman and Swinburne Islands, and Fort Wadsworth.

A SURVEY OF SOME STATEN ISLAND NEIGHBORHOODS

The North Shore—The West Shore—The East Shore—The Midline—The South Shore

Staten Islanders think of their borough as divided into four "Shores," which more or less follow the Island's geological underpinnings—outwash plain, serpentine hills, moraine, and western flatlands; they also conform more or less to the four political divisions created by the British c.1687, which became the townships of Northfield, Southfield, Westfield, and Castleton—the last named by governor Thomas Dongan (1683–88), after Cassiltowne, his estate in County Kildare, Ireland.

At first, villages developed from the shoreline inward, as topography dictated (flat land for farming, coastal and marshy areas for fishing and oystering, the hilly central area for mining and, later, for mansions with panoramic views). Later, however, these villages evolved according to their proximity to Manhattan or New Jersey and the development of ferries, roads, railroads and, eventually, highways. When the Island became a borough of New York City in 1898, the villages became neighborhoods, rather than individual towns. (The description that follows groups together the inland portions of several "Shores" as "The Midline.")

THE NORTH SHORE

The neighborhoods along the North Shore, the first to be suburbanized or industrialized, are now the most time-worn, their problems—aging housing stock, pollution, inadequate parking space, bureaucratic neglect—common to many older urban communities. These neighborhoods include the most racially mixed, the most populous, the poorest, and the most politically liberal. The North Shore declined after the Verrazano-Narrows Bridge and the Staten Island Expressway opened up the Island's midsection in the 1960s, siphoning off economic opportunity and drawing commerce to the Staten Island Mall (1973). Of the Island's eleven publicly-financed housing developments, eight are on the North Shore. On the other hand, the North Shore's assets—the historic streets and neighborhoods of Port Richmond and St. George, the Kill van Kull waterfront and its successful maritime industries, the right-of-way of the former North Shore Railroad—have attracted attention and the Department of City Planning has proposed to revitalize the area, by increasing public access to (and views of) the waterfront, developing new parks, improving transportation, cleaning up brownfields, creating a Bluebelt using the wetlands at Snug Harbor to handle storm water, and protecting the shoreline from storm surges and the erosion caused by wakes in the shipping channel. The Staten Island Ferry from Manhattan docks at St. George (*map p. 261, E1–F1*).

THE STATEN ISLAND 9/11 MEMORIAL

The destruction of the World Trade Center on 11 September 2001 affected Staten Island profoundly. More than 270 of its men and women died that day: firefighters, police officers, office workers, and employees of the Port Authority. The utter absence of the towers that once dominated the downtown skyline kept the event alive in the memory of Staten Islanders, who used to see them daily across the harbor or from the ferry—though recently the physical emptiness has been filled, as new buildings rise.

In Staten Island, the process of constructing an official memorial was remarkably swift, free of the acrimonious debates that for years plagued the effort at Ground Zero—though deciding upon a design was not easy given the many emotional, political, and religious sensibilities involved. A Memorial Advisory Committee chose Masayuki Sono's design from 179 submissions, and since 2004, the memorial, called *Postcards*, has spread its wings above a windswept plaza on the St. George Esplanade.

Sheltered within the two white wings of vinyl resin that rise from the plaza, recessed granite plaques hold silhouettes of the Staten Islanders killed in the attack, the niches often decorated with impromptu offerings. At night the site is illuminated, urban and yet isolated. For many, the spare architecture creates a symbol with universal as well as personal meaning.

St. George

St. George (*map p. 261, E1*) is the Island's downtown, its transportation hub, and the seat of borough government. The St. George Terminal of the Staten Island Ferry boasts large windows, tanks of tropical fish, and a photo mural by Michael Falco depicting the Island's watery environment (*see p. 57*). An esplanade along the Kill van Kull west of the ferry leads past the Richmond County Bank Ballpark (2001), home turf of the Staten Island Yankees, a Class-A farm club of the New York Yankees.

Up a steep hill behind the ferry terminal stand the monumental, French-influenced Borough Hall (1906) and the Richmond County Courthouse (1919), both designed by the white-glove firm of Carrère and Hastings and intended as part of a grand civic center that never got built. Nearby are the St. George Branch of the New York Public Library, the rehabbed St. George Theater (at 35 Hyatt St), and the Staten Island Museum (*see p. 219*). The St. George–New Brighton Historic District centered around St. Marks Place between Westervelt Place and Hamilton Avenue, offers a group of houses, mostly from the 1880s and 1890s, in Queen Anne, Shingle, and Colonial Revival styles, originally part of a planned suburban community.

Since the 1990s, redevelopment has given waterfront St. George new vim. Back in the 1880s, entrepreneur Erastus Wiman bought land on which to consolidate train routes and ferry lines and created the Staten Island Amusement Company à la Coney Island, to lure crowds off the ferry.

More than a century later the idea has resurfaced, as Staten Islanders mull over the prospect of erecting a Ferris wheel to dwarf all others on the present stadium parking lot.

In the lobby of **Borough Hall** (*2–10 Richmond Terrace*), a set of muscular WPA murals (1940) by Frederick Charles Stahr depicts scenes of local history: Giovanni da Verrazano, resplendent in a steel breastplate and scarlet cape, staring with wild surmise at Staten Island; Dutch colonist Cornelis Melyn bartering with the Indians (whose apparent satisfaction doesn't suggest that within the year they would massacre Melyn's band of farmers); an overdressed society couple idly watching workers on the Bayonne Bridge.

Two more sets of WPA murals are slated to be installed in the **Richmond County Supreme Court** (*18 Richmond Terrace*). The first set consists of six panels by the Chicago artist Charles Vincent Davis, who belonged to a group of young black painters committed to depicting the urban life of the Bronzeville community of African Americans on Chicago's South Side. Davis studied briefly at the Chicago Art Institute, one of the few academies at the time that admitted black students, and at Hull House, whose programs played a role in supporting socially conscious artists. The murals, entitled "The Progress of American Industry," show men plowing, mining, bridge-building, and so on. Originally painted for the craft rooms at the Farm Colony (*see p. 194*) and commissioned in 1938, the murals were to

have inspired joy and satisfaction in having contributed to
the progress of American industry—but Davis viewed the
world less rosily than did his government sponsors. He
wrote to them pointing out that these paintings, executed
in the requisite heroic Social Realist style, did not explain
why the men who had plowed, mined, laid rails, and built
bridges should be living out their final years in the poorhouse. But then, he added, perhaps the very fact that the
workers were there was sufficient commentary.

Axel Horn, a New York artist who studied at the Arts
Students' League with Thomas Hart Benton, painted the
second set, depicting the "Economic Pursuits of the Early
American Settlers." They show sturdy colonists working
in harmony with equally sturdy Native Americans, sowing
and reaping, hunting, and building a stockade.

West of St. George

Richmond Terrace, once an Indian trail, later a cow path,
now a thoroughfare, sidles along the Kill van Kull from
St. George westward to Howland Hook. Beyond the esplanade at St. George, the shore becomes industrial. Staten
Island's maritime industries—shipyards, marine transport
companies, and dry docks—still thrive on the Kill, facing what even in 1939 the *WPA Guide to New York City*
called the "desolate shore of near-by New Jersey." From the
Terrace, you can watch humongous tankers and container ships, bigger than skyscrapers toppled on their sides,
gliding by at remarkable speed, so close sometimes as to

seem within arm's reach. Further west are residential New Brighton and West Brighton.

New Brighton (*map p. 261, E1*) originated as a "romantic" planned suburban community, some of its wide, tree-lined streets laid out in 1835 by entrepreneur Thomas E. Davis to attract well-to-do commuters. Davis's own house was eventually incorporated into a hotel, the Pavilion (demolished 1904; *see p. 167*). Before and during the Civil War, Southern planters lodged their families in this and other similar hotels—one reason why many Staten Islanders remained favorably disposed toward the South. Julia Gardiner Tyler, widow of the slave-owning Virginian President John Tyler and herself an extreme advocate for slavery, aired her Confederate sympathies in the *New York Herald*, stating that slaves lived sumptuously compared to northern industrial workers. Her Greek-Revival house still stands at 27 Tyler Street.

Downhill facing the water (*561 Richmond Terrace*) stands the former factory of the J.B. King Windsor Plaster Mills, which arrived in 1876 and was later joined by the Muralo Paint Company next door (1894). In 1924, United States Gypsum bought the plaster mill, closing it 1976 because of rising production costs. Atlantic Salt, supplier of road salt for New York City streets, today occupies the land, its sterile white saline mountains creating an eerie lunar landscape (when they are visible and not covered over). The two factories typify a pattern of industrial development and then abandonment that marks the North Shore along the Kill. Corrugated metal fences crowned with razor wire, weedy vacant lots, and low factory buildings occlude the view of the water along much of Richmond Terrace.

Amid the industrial grayness, **Snug Harbor Cultural Center** astonishes like Oz after Kansas—green lawns, mature trees, a fountain, and architecture so finely proportioned that even the unrestored brick rear walls draw your eye. Once a home for retired merchant mariners, today it is the focus of Staten Island art and culture. Among its riches are the Noble Maritime Collection, the Chinese Scholar's Garden, the Newhouse Center for Contemporary Art, the Staten Island Children's Museum, the Music Hall, and artists' studios. It's hard to believe that Snug Harbor was once slated to be bulldozed in favor of housing. Like many other good things on Staten Island, it owes its life to tenacious preservationists. (*For more on Snug Harbor and the Noble Maritime Collection, see pp. 61 and 70.*)

Before the Civil War, Abolitionists from New England settled in **West Brighton** (*map p. 261, D1–D2*), energized by a moral intensity that was at odds with the attitudes of their Confederate-leaning neighbors. One of the leaders was George William Curtis, an essayist, publisher, and Unitarian of staunch New England heritage (his house still stands at 234 Bard Avenue). Curtis and his fellow activists propagandized non-stop, produced an anti-slavery newspaper, supported the election of Abraham Lincoln, and operated a station of the Underground Railway. Curtis

married the sister of Robert Gould Shaw, who commanded a black regiment in the Civil War and died at the Battle
of Fort Wagner in South Carolina in 1863.

Mandolin Brothers, which dates back to 1971 (*see overleaf*), occupies an unlikely yellowish stucco-faced building
at 629 Forest Avenue.

Further west, on flat land at the confluence of the Kill van
Kull and the Arthur Kill, are **Port Richmond** and **Mariners
Harbor** (*map p. 260, C1–C2*), important as transportation
links, first for the colonial ferries that made Staten Island
a leg of the most efficient route between New York and
points south, and more recently for the Bayonne and Goethals Bridges. The mansion of governor Thomas Dongan
(d.1715) stood on Richmond Terrace between present-day
Dongan and Bodine Streets, across from what is now a water pollution control plant. Nineteenth-century captains of
clippers and oyster ships built mansions facing the water:
the Stephen D. Barnes House (*2876 Richmond Terrace, between Van Pelt and Van Name Aves*), built in 1853, is the
sole survivor of "Captain's Row." In 1836, Aaron Burr, best
known for killing Alexander Hamilton in a duel, spent the
declining weeks of his life in a boarding house (*site of 2040
Richmond Terrace, near Port Richmond Ave*) and died there.
His obituary in Baltimore's *Niles' Weekly Register* remarked
that "all admired him for the bravery and talents that ren-
dered him such an important auxiliary in the early struggles of our country, and lamented that they were perverted
by unhallowed ambition."

MANDOLIN BROTHERS

Most off-islanders know Staten Island for the ferry, the bridge, or the (former) Fresh Kills dump, but a certain crowd knows it as the home of Mandolin Brothers, reputedly "the best guitar shop in New York and probably the universe." It is the place where Joni Mitchell went to buy herself a mandolin back in 1976. Actually she didn't buy a mandolin; she bought a mandocello, which is to a mandolin what a cello is to a violin. Had she wanted to, she could have purchased a mandola (the viola of the mandolin family) or a mandobass, or even a shining National guitar. Instead she contented herself with a Gibson K-4 mandocello built c.1915 and a Martin 000-28 herringbone guitar of the same vintage. In "Song for Sharon," which she began on the ferry ride back to Manhattan, Mitchell rhymes "mandolin" with "mannequin," but, as Stan Jay the affable and knowledgeable owner of Mandolin Brothers points out, you'd be hard pressed to find meaningful rhymes for "mandocello."

Mandolin Brothers has drawn players, singers, and composers from all over the world; luminaries include George Benson, Bob Dylan, George Harrison, the Indigo Girls, Pat Metheny, and Paul Simon, as well as a smattering of famous chefs, comedians, journalists, and attorneys. The store's repair shop re-intonated Paul McCartney's Hofner bass to the satisfaction of the former Beatle, who remarked that it had never played in tune before.

Before the consequences of heavy industry became clear, Port Richmond took pride in its industrial muscle, but the once-vaunted factories have departed, leaving behind a residue of ecological distress and economic decline. The Jewett White Lead and Linseed Oil Company stood on Richmond Terrace near Heberton Street; other nearby factories manufactured fireworks, varnishes, and dyes, or stockpiled scrap metal. Beginning in 1907, at Port Ivory (now Howland Hook), Procter & Gamble manufactured Ivory soap, synthetic detergents, and hydrogenated vegetable oils (i.e. Crisco). Bethlehem Steel's shipbuilding works turned out destroyers during World War II and ferries thereafter. But one by one these plants closed, lured elsewhere by lower production costs, cheaper labor, better transportation, or more acreage. A railroad once served the North Shore, but passenger service was discontinued in 1953, isolating the western reaches of the shoreline.

South and east of St. George

Tompkinsville (*map p. 261, E1*), site of "the Watering Place," where outbound ships in colonial days filled their casks, was the Island's oldest village; it dates to about 1817 when Daniel D. Tompkins started a steam ferry service to Manhattan. Tompkins served as New York State governor (1807–17) and vice-president of the US (1817–25). As governor he loaned his own capital to the state for military expenditures, but the endless litigation he undertook to recover the money ruined his health. Today Tompkinsville is urban and multi-ethnic, with a population of Italians, blacks, and Latin Americans, as well as a large group of Sri Lankans near Bay Street.

Stapleton along with **Clifton** (*map p. 261, E2*) became Staten Island's beer capital. German immigrants established breweries, taking advantage of the natural springs and cool hillside caves to produce and store lager. The best-known firms were the Bachmann Brewery (1853) and the Rubsam and Hormann Atlantic Brewery (1871), which was bought by Piels and lasted until 1963.

BAYLEY-SETON HOSPITAL

Bayley-Seton Hospital (*75 Vanderbilt Ave; the landmarked building is visible from Bay St; map p. 261, F2*) began as the Seaman's Retreat, founded in 1831 to care for sick and disabled merchant sailors. Unlike Sailors' Snug Harbor, which was financed by a charitable bequest, the Seaman's Retreat was funded by a state tax levied on mariners entering the harbor. The first hospital building was a converted farmhouse whose site had been selected by a committee that included four sea captains, but by 1837 the present landmarked building was completed and by 1870 it had been expanded to include flanking wings around the central pavilion. The sailors were treated for broken bones, venereal diseases, arthritis, even for diarrhea (understandably common among seamen considering shipboard food and lack of refrigeration). Men who were chronically ill and had nowhere to go could stay for months or even years.

For a while there was plenty of money. But, according to a *New York Times* story in 1873, Cornelius Vanderbilt declared the head tax unconstitutional (a dollar per man per voyage) and refused to let his mariners pay it. Vanderbilt's allies followed suit, and by 1882, the Retreat, in financial distress, was sold to the Marine Society (already active at Sailors' Snug Harbor). They leased the building to the federal government, who closed the Retreat and moved a US Marine Hospital there from Bedloe's (now Liberty) Island, giving the Statue of Liberty room to raise her torch. In 1903, the government bought the hospital and added land purchased from the Vanderbilts in 1931, completing the site of what became a US Public Health Service Hospital. Today those buildings dominate the site.

In 1981, the government left and the Sisters of Charity took over, naming the institution for Dr. Richard Bayley (1745–1801) and his daughter, St. Elizabeth Ann Seton (*see p. 140*). Bayley died of yellow fever contracted in the line of duty while head of the Quarantine. Since 2000, the hospital has gone through several changes of ownership. It still offers inpatient psychiatric services but its future is uncertain.

South of Clifton is small-town, short-streeted **Rosebank** (*map p. 261, F2*), also shaped by its immigrant heritage. In the 1880s and 1890s Rosebank saw an influx of southern Italians, whose descendants remain the predominant ethnic group, though the neighborhood is becoming increasingly diverse with Poles, West Africans, Asians and Mexicans. The US Quarantine was long located here. The Alice Austen House (*see p. 126*) by the water reflects the graciousness of an earlier time. The Garibaldi-Meucci Museum (*see p. 183*) recalls the Italian hero's brief stay on Staten Island. Hidden away on little Amity Street is the grotto of Our Lady of Mount Carmel (*see p. 184*), a remarkable example of devotional art. At the southern end of Rosebank, Fort Wadsworth (*see p. 169*), a bulwark in the Island's military history, overlooks the Narrows.

THE WEST SHORE

The settlements of the West Shore long remained quietly rural, the province of truck farmers who raised strawberries, asparagus, sweet potatoes, and other crops that thrived in sandy soil. During the summer of 1922, Harlem Renaissance poet Langston Hughes, abandoning his life as a student at Columbia University, worked on a small farm owned by a Greek family in **Bulls Head** (*map p. 260, C3*), growing onions.

The West Shore also served as the departure point for ferries crossing the Arthur Kill to New Jersey. **Travis** (*map *p. 260, B3*), where the New Blazing Star Ferry to Perth Amboy docked during the eighteenth century, continued in its small-town ways until the mid-twentieth century.

In 1948, Robert Moses "temporarily" designated **Fresh Kills** as the final resting place of New York City's garbage; the West Shore Expressway made the area accessible and opened the eyes of developers to economic opportunity. As one ecological disgrace followed hard on another—air pollution, water pollution, destruction of wetlands, over-building on inadequate infrastructure—the landscape was unalterably changed. Today the former landfill is being recycled as Freshkills Park (*see p. 124*).

Rossville (*map p. 262, B5*), small and remote and the site of a ferry to New Jersey, was settled early, farmed into the nineteenth century, orphaned by rapid transit in the early twentieth century, and encrusted with suburban homes after the arrival of the West Shore Expressway in the mid-1970s. The town is named after businessman William E. Ross, whose home, "Ross Castle," said to have been a replica of Windsor Castle, overlooked the Kill. The population today includes Italians, Russians, and Jews, as well as Asians. Along the Arthur Kill are two small but historic cemeteries, as well as a marine salvage yard and several nineteenth-century houses, along with newer additions.

Between Rossville and Charleston, Sandy Ground (*see p. 78*), the remnant of an oystering community founded by free blacks from Maryland, was centered on Bloomingdale Road (*map p. 262, A5–B5*).

THE ARTHUR KILL SALVAGE YARD

Just off the Rossville shoreline, where the Arthur Kill bends toward the road (*map p. 262, A5*), a collection of derelict ships rusts and rots in a shallow cove. It is Staten Island's largest remaining ships' graveyard, or boneyard, formerly the Witte Marine Equipment Company. Now it is part of the Donjon Marine Company, whose business includes salvage and wreck removal, towing, barge chartering, and pollution prevention. The first proprietor of the salvage yard, John J. Witte (d. 1980), preferred not to break up the ships in his yard until he found buyers for their parts. As more and more were towed here and abandoned, the place became a repository of maritime history, with the oldest ships closest to shore and more recent arrivals further out in the water. There were ferries, steamboats, fireboats, even sailing ships and side-wheelers, vestiges of the days when hulls were wood and ships were propelled by sail or steam. They lay at odd angles, smokestacks tilted, wheelhouses collapsing, hulls sinking into the mud. The old fleet is disappearing ever more quickly as the shoreline is developed, and shipworms, once deterred by pollution, are making a comeback in cleaner water.

John A. Noble (*see p. 70*) sketched the dying ships, though John Witte, fierce about visitors, kicked him out so often that he finally quit coming. Today photographers and artists are still drawn to the spot, attracted by the melancholy of derelict places whose past life lingers. The salvage yard does not welcome visitors.

THE EAST SHORE

Grasmere, a pleasant residential neighborhood of houses and condos, lies west of Fort Wadsworth and east of the central hills (*map p. 261, E2*). Within its boundaries are freshwater Brady Pond and the home office of the *Staten Island Advance*. Sir Roderick Cameron (1823–1900), a Canadian-born shipping magnate with an interest in horse breeding, gave the neighborhood its name, borrowed from an English village whose most famous resident was William Wordsworth. Cameron began modestly as a clerk in a dry goods store, but embarked on a more exciting and lucrative career during the Australian gold rush when he chartered a ship to carry passengers and supplies from New York to Australia. His obituary in the *New York Times* notes that, true to his acquired class, he drank vintage champagne and tawny port, and dined on Stilton cheese and roast beef.

The beach towns of the East Shore, **South Beach**, **Midland Beach** and **New Dorp** (*map p. 261, E4–F3*), bookended by two chunks of the Gateway National Recreation Area, share a common history, developing from farming and fishing communities, to resorts of beach colonies with hotels, tents, or bungalows, to their present status as middle-class waterside neighborhoods. All have significant Italian American populations, though like the rest of Staten Island, all are becoming more ethnically diverse. In 2012, the twelve-foot storm surge following Hurricane

Sandy wrenched former cottages off their foundations, swept away walls, and filled ground-floor businesses ceiling deep.

ANGELS' CIRCLE

In the traffic triangle where Hylan Boulevard meets Fingerboard Road, Angels' Circle (*map p. 261, F2*) stands as a "people's memorial" to 9/11. It began as an impromptu outpouring, but has remained intact, indeed has flourished, in the years since 2001. After the planes hit the Towers, a resident of the neighborhood, Wendy Pellegrino, planted a flag and a hand-lettered sign, "God Bless Our Heroes," on the traffic island. From that seed, the memorial grew until today it looks as if a flight of assorted angels has alighted on the site. Cherubic or mourning, wings spread or folded, large and small, they stand among rows of memorial cards interspersed with candles, religious images, rosaries, poems, and objects of personal significance. A local florist tends the plantings with help from neighborhood volunteers. At night the circle is illuminated; a memorial service takes place annually on September 11, and at Christmas, in accordance with Staten Island tradition, the intersection becomes a feast of lights.

South Beach occupies the site of Oude Dorp, Staten Island's original Dutch settlement of 1661. Long an Italian neighborhood, it today also has an affluent community of

Russians. Midland Beach, just to the south of Old Dorp, was known in the nineteenth century for resort hotels, theaters, Ferris wheels, shooting galleries, bathing pavilions, and beer gardens, some sponsored by the German breweries of Stapleton and Clifton. The beach and amusements attracted as many as 40,000 weekend visitors from stifling New York. Eventually the resorts succumbed to fire, water pollution, and economic downturn; the City took over the dilapidated beachfront in 1935 and constructed the 2½-mile Franklin Delano Roosevelt (FDR) Boardwalk, from the southern end of Fort Wadsworth to Miller Field. Visible offshore are Hoffman (the larger) and Swinburne Islands (*see p. 21*).

New Dorp was settled in 1671 by Dutch, French, and English farmers and fishermen. The Vanderbilt family had large land holdings, and from 1842 until 1863, part of William H. Vanderbilt's farm occupied what is now Miller Field, site of the Elm Tree Lighthouse. Part of New Dorp lies on sandy lowland close to the beach, but the neighborhood also reaches inland to hilly Moravian Cemetery.

The Moravian Cemetery

The Moravian Cemetery (*map p. 261, D3*) occupies 113 acres of landscaped knolls, hills, and meadows on the southeast flank of Todt Hill. It is owned by the United Brethren, whose white steepled church (1844) and earlier Dutch-Colonial style building (1763) stand near the entrance from Todt Hill Road.

Although the Native Americans had buried their dead in graves marked only with shells, anonymity in death disappeared with the arrival of Europeans. The Dutch, who were predominantly farmers, had buried their dead in homestead graveyards, often in the remote corners of their fields, marking the graves with stones or wooden planks, fencing the plots to keep out livestock. Itinerant carvers sometimes inscribed the stones with mottos, symbols of death or life, and the names and dates of the deceased, and some of these eighteenth-century tombstones still stand, bearing winged death heads—terrifying images of skulls with bared, Chiclet-shaped teeth—graceful willow-and-urn designs, or winged cherubs, a gentler variation worked on the death's-head theme.

Churchyard cemeteries came into existence during the eighteenth century. The Moravian, whose earliest gravestone dates to c. 1740, may first have been a public burial ground, but later served members of the nearby church. Bodies were initially buried with their feet toward the east, since it was believed that "the Lord would come on the sunrise at the resurrection." The pastors of the congregation, however, were buried facing west in order to face their flock when they all arose. Early graves were marked with flat marble slabs, since in death all are equal, but later grave markers reflected social status: the souls may have been equal in death, but the monuments are not.

Part of the cemetery's original land belonged to governor Thomas Dongan, some of whose relatives rest here.

Later the Vanderbilts, members of the Moravian Church, extended their generosity; Cornelius Vanderbilt donated more than fifty acres, to which his son William H. Vanderbilt added another four, as well as a parsonage and a superintendent's house. He contributed to the building of the cemetery's Central Avenue, which winds from the southwestern entrance up the hill to the present Vanderbilt family plot.

Among those buried in the Moravian Cemetery are at least eighty-nine Civil War veterans (though not Robert Gould Shaw, who is memorialized by a cenotaph) and forty-five men and women who died on 11 September 2001; abolitionist and writer George William Curtis and his wife Anna Shaw Curtis; photographer Alice Austen (*see p. 126*); landscapist Jasper Francis Cropsey; Thomas Melville (*see p. 67*); reputed mob boss Paul ("Big Paulie") Castellano (*see p. 187*) and his reputed heir-apparent Thomas Bilotti; cigar maker Alvaro Garcia; pencil maker Eberhard Faber; beer maker August Hormann; and architect John M. Carrère. William T. Davis (*see p. 99*) and his co-author Charles W. Leng are also here, as is Stephen Weed, who died at Gettysburg on 2 July 1863, and for whom the battery at Fort Wadsworth is named. Film maker Martin Scorsese (b. 1942) has reserved a plot.

At the northern edge of the Moravian Cemetery, in an expansive private enclosure, stands the **Vanderbilt Mausoleum**. There is no public access to the monument, but its entrance gates are visible. (*For the story of the Mauso-*

leum, its fortunes and misfortunes, and more on the family that built it and their connection to Staten Island, see p. 141.)

THE MIDLINE
(NORTH, EAST, & WEST SHORES INLAND)

Along the Island's rocky midline, well-to-do neighborhoods arose during the early years of the nineteenth century, established by New Yorkers seeking relief from urban crowding and Southerners seeking relief from the heat. Suzette Grymes, widow of Louisiana's first governor and thereafter wife of a wealthy and eccentric New Orleans lawyer, arrived in 1836 and built her mansion, "Capodimonte," on the hill that bears her name (**Grymes Hill**; *map p. 261, E2*). Historians Leng and Davis describe her as a "strong masculine woman," her son-in-law's biographer calls her "a fortune-hunting shrew," but her obituary, published in New Orleans, describes her as "beautiful and accomplished, superbly endowed by nature and charmingly cultivated." Other wealthy nineteenth-century homeowners nearby included Sir Edward Cunard and Jacob H. Vanderbilt, brother of the Commodore.

Emerson Hill, off Ocean Terrace, got its name from the brother of Ralph Waldo Emerson, William, who lived here from 1837 until 1864; he hired Henry David Thoreau to tutor his children, a job that may have quashed Thoreau's remaining ambitions as a teacher (*see p. 103*). **Dongan Hills** is named for colonial governor Thomas Dongan.

Todt Hill (*map p. 261, D3*) was called "Iron Hill" (Yserberg) by the Dutch, who mined iron in the vicinity. (The origin of *todt*, "dead" in German, is uncertain.) Architect Ernest Flagg built his mansion, "Stone Court" (*209 Flagg Place*), in 1898. Flagg was interested in model tenements and hotels for the poor as well as homes and commercial buildings for the rich: later he put up modest stone cottages adjacent to the mansion and, in 1925, a "demonstration house" (*1929 Richmond Road*) for *McCall's Magazine* as an example of economy, convenience, and the benefits of modern technology. Today Stone Court houses the St. Charles Mission Center and the Center for Migration Studies. The "Godfather House" (*see p. 189*) and former Mafia boss Paul Castellano's mansion (*see p. 187*) are in this neighborhood.

On **Lighthouse Hill**, between Edinboro Road and Manor Court (*map p. 261, D4*), stands the beautiful Staten Island Range Light (*see p. 92*), a pale brick octagonal tower and a startling presence in the midst of an ordinary residential neighborhood. Nearby is the Jacques Marchais Museum of Tibetan Art (*see p. 134*).

Further south is **Richmond** (*map p. 261, D4*), Staten Island's seat of government and principal commercial center before the Island joined New York City. Today it is Historic Richmond Town, a museum village, whose restored buildings outline the borough's history from the seventeenth through the nineteenth centuries.

Historic Richmond Town

The redoubtable William T. Davis (*see p. 99*) and Loring McMillen, the unpaid borough historian for fifty-four years, spearheaded the effort to save Staten Island's architectural past, restoring and relocating endangered buildings and eventually establishing the museum village. On a weekend hike in 1929, McMillen (then twenty-three) chanced to meet Davis (then sixty-seven), leading a group on one of his "tramps," dressed in his usual dark suit and straw boater hat. Over the years Davis became McMillen's mentor, and the two continued exploring, unearthing old foundations, and collecting for the Staten Island Historical Society, of which Davis was president. They called on families who lived in old houses and asked about the contents of attics. One source reports that an elderly woman repaid McMillen, who pulled her goat out of a well, giving him an old plow and an ice marker formerly used to mark blocks of ice in a pond for cutting. During the Depression, a WPA project furthered the work by hiring historians and archaeologists to document significant buildings and interview older Islanders. In 1937, the Voorlezer's House, then in ruins, was recognized for what it was (*see below*); its restoration sparked a plan for an outdoor museum. By 1948, five historic structures, including the Second County Courthouse (1793) and the Third County Courthouse (1837), formed the nucleus of the village. In 1952, Robert Moses engineered purchase of the land; six years later Historic Richmond Town was founded.

In the village are modest Dutch Colonial houses, a clap-boarded Gothic Revival house with jig-sawed gingerbread on the eaves, and examples of Italianate and Queen Anne styles of vernacular architecture. The oldest building is the Britton Cottage (c. 1670 with additions), ancestral home of botanist Nathaniel Lord Britton (*see p. 96*). The most historically significant is the Voorlezer's House (c. 1695) thought to be the earliest schoolhouse in the US. The *voor-lezer* (lay reader), hired in place of a full-time preacher, combined the hortatory duties of teaching school and leading religious services. The grandest building is the Greek Revival Third County Courthouse, built in 1837 when Staten Island was becoming a significant suburb. The humblest buildings are two outhouses, or privies, dating to the latter half of the nineteenth century. One is small and ordinary, the other a veritable Versailles of outhouses, originally a two-room, six-seater.

Across Richmond Road is Dunn's Mill, a former grist mill, whose pond has been reconstructed as part of the Staten Island Bluebelt (*see p. 147*) program.

The present stone **Church of St. Andrew** on the outskirts of Historic Richmond Town (*40 Old Mill Road; map p. 261, D4*) was built in 1872, though the congregation dates back to 1708, founded by the Reverend Aeneas MacKenzie, who had been sent as a missionary by the Society for the Propagation of the Gospel in Foreign Parts. MacKenzie established two schools in the neighborhood, hiring teachers "to instruct the poor whites, and black children also, if any such are brought to him, gratis." Parts of the stone walls of the original building are incorporated in the present structure. During the Revolution the British had a camp nearby, and several skirmishes were fought near the church, which served as a hospital for wounded British soldiers. The historic cemetery contains graves of early Staten Islanders, including Dr. Richard Bayley, father of St. Elizabeth Ann Seton.

THE SOUTH SHORE

Reaching from Great Kills Park south to Tottenville, and along the Arthur Kill up to Rossville and inland to Richmond, the South Shore embraces the southern part of the terminal moraine and the surrounding flatlands. This part of the Island remained rural until well after the opening of the Verrazano-Narrows Bridge in 1964, and the onslaught of new construction arrived only in the 1980s, after land further north had been developed. Some of Staten Island's best parks and natural areas are here.

Great Kills Park's 580 acres of beachfront and coastal wetlands (*map p. 263, E4*) constitute one of the city's finest ecological preserves. John J. Crooke, for whom a sandy spit of land is named, was a businessman with mining interests in Colorado and a tinfoil factory in New York. An enthusiastic naturalist, he bought land here in 1860 and camped on it, collecting specimens of plants, shells, and birds, some of which later found their way to the Staten Island Museum, the American Museum of Natural History, and the New York Botanical Garden. In the 1920s, a developer hankered to turn the point into a residential colony with an amusement park; during the Depression the City bought the land and used it for a dump, filling the salt marsh with trash and burying it under clay and sludge from city sewage plants; in 1949, the City opened Great Kills as a park; in 1973, the federal government included it in the Gateway National Recreation Area.

Prince's Bay (*map p. 262, B6*), a community whose early economy was based on oystering and agriculture, still retains a few houses from its shell-fishing heyday, for example, the John H. and Elizabeth J. Elsworth House (1879) near the train station (*90 Bayview Ave*), and the Abraham J. Wood House of 1840 (*5910 Amboy Road*).

Lemon Creek Park (*Hylan Blvd from Sharrott Ave to Seguine Ave; map p. 262, B6*) has 105 acres of relatively undisturbed salt- and freshwater marsh, a tidal creek emptying into Prince's Bay, oak forests, a freshwater pond, and New York City's only purple martin colony, housed in elaborately architectural birdhouses.

Overlooking a broad lawn sweeping down to Prince's Bay, the imposing Greek Revival **Joseph H. Seguine House** (*440 Seguine Ave*) suggests the wealth of Staten Island's oystering families during the high tide of that industry. It was built in 1838 by Joseph Seguine, of French Huguenot ancestry, who founded the Staten Island Oil and Candlemaking company on the property, harvested salt hay, and served as first president of the Staten Island Railroad. The Seguine family planted the Osage orange trees along the avenue at the suggestion of Frederick Law Olmsted, who lived nearby (*see p. 107*). In 1981, designer George Burke, who fondly remembered the place from his childhood, bought the derelict house and restored it, eventually ceding it to the city.

Joseph H. Seguine was born nearby in the Manee-Seguine House (*509 Seguine Ave*), now a derelict, endangered survivor surrounded by weeds, trash trees, and chain link fencing. The oldest part dates back to about 1670, built by one Paulus Regrenier, who operated a lime kiln for burning oyster shells; Abraham Manee, also a Huguenot, added a rubble-stone wing; the Seguine family contributed a two-story wood-frame addition.

The **Memorial Church of the Huguenots** (aka the Reformed Church of Huguenot Park; *5475 Amboy Rd.; map p. 262, B6*) commemorates the tercentenary of the arrival of Huguenots in New Netherland. Architect Ernest Flagg, who traced his own Anglo-French heritage back to the twelfth century and considered himself a latter-day Huguenot, built the church to recall the Romanesque architecture of Normandy, Brittany, and England. The building expresses not only Flagg's personal brand of medievalism, but his interest in economical building techniques. The stonework of the façade, for example, was constructed by placing fieldstones in a re-usable structural form and then pouring concrete around them, precluding the need for skilled masons. Built in 1924, the church belongs to Flagg's series of experimental stone buildings constructed with serpentinite quarried from his own estate.

The principal point of interest in the suburban neighborhood of **Pleasant Plains** is the **Mount Loretto Unique Area** (*map p. 262, B7*), a 194-acre nature preserve of freshwater and tidal wetlands, grassland, and forest, formerly the grounds of a Catholic orphanage and school. Father John Drumgoole, who founded the Mission of the Immaculate Virgin, devoted his pastoral life to caring for destitute children, establishing (1870) a lodging house in Manhattan for homeless newsboys, and moving the mission to Staten Island ten years later when it outgrew its building (homeless newsboys were abundant at the end of the nineteenth century). The Mission, which operated a farm and a trade school, cared for and educated thousands of children before it closed in the 1990s. The property offers spectacular views from its three hiking trails.

Within the preserve is the former **Prince's Bay Lighthouse** (renamed the John Cardinal O'Connor Lighthouse in 2007), which stands on 85-foot red clay bluffs that mark the limit of the terminal moraine of the last Wisconsin Glacier. Built in 1864 to replace an earlier rubblestone version, the sturdy brownstone tower with its attached keeper's house was deactivated in 1922 when navigation lights were placed in Raritan Bay. Four years later, the Archdiocese of New York bought the house and tower at auction to consolidate the grounds of the Mission. In 1953, a small automated rear range light was established near the deactivated tower with the front range light 45 yards away on the beach.

On the grounds of the mission is the Church of St. Joachim and St. Anne, also founded by Father Drumgoole; it burned in 1973 leaving the façade intact. Services are no longer held there, but the 205-foot tower still soars above the flatlands of Pleasant Plains.

Charleston (*map p. 262, A6*), along the Arthur Kill between Sandy Ground and Tottenville, was formerly called Kreischerville, for Balthazar Kreischer, whose factory (1854–1927) produced heat-resistant bricks using the clay deposited by the retreating glacier. Kreischer, an immigrant from Bavaria, built a pair of remarkable Stick-Style mansions for his sons, one of which still stands at 4500 Arthur Kill Road. On Kreischer Street, near Androvette Street, he constructed more modest houses for his workers. **Clay Pit Ponds State Park** (*83 Nielsen Ave, near Sharrotts Rd and Carlin Rd*) is a 260-acre natural area with wetlands, ponds, sand barrens, spring-fed streams and woodlands on the site of former clay mines. Two colors of Kreischer brick ornament the former Westfield Township School No. 7 (*4212 Arthur Kill Rd*).

Tottenville, at the southwest tip of the Island (*map p. 262, A7*), is the end of the line on the Staten Island Railroad and the last exit on the West Shore Expressway. It is the neighborhood furthest from Manhattan, physically about twenty miles, culturally a whole lot farther. Its remoteness has helped it keep some of its small-town atmosphere. Originally, its industries were agriculture, fishing and maritime trades. In the mid- to late-nineteenth century, industrial pollution and sewage began to impact the oyster industry, and in 1916, the New York Department of Health declared Staten Island clams and oysters unsafe. The introduction of steel-hulled ships ruined Tottenville's wooden-ship-building industry. The Atlantic Terra Cotta Works, producer of architectural decoration (most notably the Gothic appurtenances of the Woolworth Building in Manhattan) came and went (1897–c. 1935), brought down by the Depression and the change in building styles, as did the Tottenville Copper Company (1900), which became Nassau Smelting and Refining Company and was sold to Western Electric in 1931. The New York City sewer system reached Tottenville in 1994, allowing developers to put up single- and multiple-family houses without having to pay for sewage treatment facilities; thereafter suburban houses sprang up like the proverbial dragons' teeth. Nevertheless, Tottenville still has a Main Street with nineteenth-century houses, many built by families connected with the oystering industry, as well as its own historical society, an indicator of its sense of pride.

MARITIME STATEN ISLAND

The Staten Island Ferry—Sailors' Snug Harbor—John A. Noble, Salvage Artist—The Oysters of Staten Island—Sandy Ground—Staten Island Lighthouses

Ever since navigators Giovanni da Verrazano and Henry Hudson "discovered" and named it, Staten Island has been linked to the sea. If not symbolically wedded to the Atlantic like Venice to the Adriatic, it has at least enjoyed the benefits of a long and fruitful relationship. Its ferries, its maritime industries, its former seaside resorts and present coastal parks, its waterside fortifications for the defense of New York harbor, and its charities for sailors and their families all exist because of the proximity of the ocean; and huge ships still traverse the Kill van Kull and the Arthur Kill en route to Port Newark, a major shipping hub. On the northern and western coasts of the Island, dry docks and other facilities for ship repair and construction, and marine salvage companies keep alive industries established generations ago.

ICON OF THE ISLAND:
THE STATEN ISLAND FERRY

The half-hour 5.2-mile trip between Whitehall Street on Manhattan's southern tip and St. George on Staten

Island is probably the world's most famous ferry ride—after Charon's journey across the Styx. Unlike the Stygian crossing, however, the Staten Island Ferry is free, and it's round-trip. "The Boat," as Staten Islanders call it, is New York City's second most popular tourist attraction after the Statue of Liberty, carrying some 21 million passengers every year. It is also a symbol of the Island, part of its daily life and of its cultural heritage.

Why the ferry's fame? The view, of course. As you head for Manhattan from Staten Island, you pass by the stubby Robbins Reef Lighthouse (*see p. 86*); the Statue of Liberty, her right arm brandishing a torch that prefigures all the spires ahead; Ellis Island, through whose doors more than 12 million immigrants entered the United States; and, on the New Jersey side, the smaller spires and arches of the former New Jersey Central Railroad Terminal, whose ferries carried commuters to downtown Manhattan. From a distance, the towers of the downtown skyline seem to rise directly from the water, though when you get closer, you can see the patch of Battery Park at the waterline. Years ago most of the skyscrapers peaked in temples, pyramids, and other architectural fripperies that concealed water tanks and elevator machinery, but because of changes in zoning laws, most of the newer towers are boxy, as if flattened from above. Missing except in memory are the Twin Towers that in their day rose higher than the others, symbols of the commercial might of the city and the nation. If you ever saw the Twin Towers, you cannot forget where once they stood and how they looked, even though a taller tower, sleek and prismatic, has risen to replace them.

The southbound trip toward Staten Island is less dramatic than the Manhattan-bound leg, but you can stand at the ferry's stern and watch the skyscrapers of Lower Manhattan recede into the distance, their angles softening, their colors fading as the water gap widens. You can admire Castle Williams (1811) on Governors Island, and the Brooklyn waterfront, or you can look forward, as the St. George Terminal approaches, its stylized arch curving above it. To its right are the light stanchions of the Richmond County Bank Baseball Stadium and the official borough 9/11 Memorial (*see p. 25*). In the near distance rise the low hills of Staten Island, modest in comparison with the skyscrapers at your back. But then, much of Staten Island is low key.

But it's not just the view that makes the ferry memorable. It's also the journey. The ride may begin and end with crowds of hustling humanity (an average of 65,000 passengers a day, and during rush hours people push to get on the boat and shove to get off) but on the water, there's not much to do. You can read, sleep, eat, fiddle with your favorite electronic device, or watch the seagulls trailing hungrily astern. The complications of the city fall away in the boat's wake. It's a half-hour respite from the world.

WHERE MARSH MEETS THE SEA

Where Marsh Meets the Sea (2007), a glass photo mural by Michael Falco installed near the pedestrian entrance of the St. George Terminal, celebrates Staten Island's closeness to the sea. Images of bridges, boats, marsh grass, and birds fade into one another, surrounding a photograph of John A. Noble (*see p. 70*) and his two sons exploring the Island's waterways in their rowboat.

Ferry history

Ferries established by European settlers crossed the East River as early as 1642, but generations earlier Staten Island's Native Americans, the Lenape, had crossed the kills and New York Bay by canoe, establishing routes that the Dutch would follow. The first public Staten Island-to-Manhattan service began by 1708, and by 1780 ten ferry lines made the crossings to New Jersey, Brooklyn, and Manhattan in boats powered by sail, oar, and setting pole. The best-known craft were periaugers, flat-bottomed, single- or double-masted boats that could also be rowed or poled, swift but not stable. In the early nineteenth century, urcapitalist Cornelius Vanderbilt (*see p. 141*) began his own journey with a single periauger, first his father's, then his own. He spent his adolescence haunting the docks; even as a teenager he showed his competitive mettle and strategic capacities, imposing his own rules, commanding his own boat, and setting his own fares. T.J. Stiles, in his fine biography *The First Tycoon*, points out that Vanderbilt ran his ferry by a regular schedule (unlike his competitors, who waited for a full load before departing) and in his zeal to outstrip his rivals set the tone for the ferry business for the next century. By 1811 or 1812, when he was fourteen or fifteen years old, Vanderbilt was buying up shares in other men's boats and salting away the profits to enlarge his empire. By 1838, he owned the Staten Island Ferry Company.

Steam supplanted sail in 1817, and by 1857 big double-enders were making the crossing. Other ferry lines crossed the Arthur Kill to Perth Amboy and Elizabeth, and the Kill van Kull to Bayonne; still others departed Staten Island's eastern shore bound for Manhattan and Brooklyn. The business of running steam boats became a high-stakes, ego-fueled game, with ship captains recklessly racing, dueling on the water and sometimes crashing.

In addition to being dangerous, as Frederick Law Olmsted pointed out in 1871, the boats were uncomfortable, badly ventilated, badly lighted, and understaffed. The year Olmsted published his critique, the boiler of the wooden-hulled side-wheeler *Westfield II* exploded at the Whitehall dock, killing perhaps 93 and injuring 113 (the exact figures are uncertain). Cornelius Vanderbilt's brother Jacob, whose Staten Island Transit Company owned the boat, was indicted for homicide, but managed to avoid conviction. The *Westfield II* was repaired and put back into service, though she was later demoted to the late-night run carrying milk wagons and at the end of her life was assigned to redemptive hospital duty transporting the sick.

A poem about three boats, the *Wave*, the *Samson*, and the *Hercules*, which appeared in the *Richmond County Mirror* (and is quoted by Leng and Davis in their history of Staten Island), expresses popular discontent with the ferry service:

> To the *Wave*
> He who would a sixpence save
> Must join the rabble on the *Wave*
>
> The *Wave's* Reply
> He who would avoid a squeeze
> Must patronize the *Hercu-lees*
> Ye, who would sink lower still
> Try the *Samson*—but make your will
> *"A plague on both your houses"*—Shaks.

Thirty years after the *Westfield II* disaster, in June 1901, the *Northfield*, while pulling out of its slip at Whitehall, was struck by the Jersey Central Railroad's *Mauch Chunk* and sank. Some of the hotly competitive spirit seems to have survived in that collision, since the rival companies were quarreling over use of the Manhattan slips. In the trial that followed the sinking, the jury censored the captain of the *Mauch Chunk* for running full steam ahead near the slip and failing to reverse its engines for the *Northfield*, which had the right of way. The jury exonerated the captain of the *Northfield*, and recommended legislation regulating the speed of boats as they docked.

Partly because of the *Northfield* crash, the City took control of the ferries in 1905, adding five new boats to the fleet and over time implementing safety measures. The boats were painted barn red to make them visible in the fog; today they are bright orange, like traffic cones and flotation vests. In 1908, a rule stipulated that two pilots capable of managing the boat should be in the wheelhouse as the ferry docked, a rule whose non-observance led to tragedy a century later.

In 2003, the ill-fated *Andrew J. Barberi* slammed full speed into a maintenance pier near its Staten Island slip, splintering the wooden pilings. As momentum carried the ferry forward, the concrete pier ripped through the starboard cabin of the main deck, killing eleven people. The assistant captain, alone in the wheelhouse despite regulations to the contrary, confessed to having lost consciousness as the boat approached the dock. Although lawyers for the City asserted that the crash was an act of God, the court later judged the assistant captain and his supervisor guilty of manslaughter, the former for operating the boat while impaired—he took painkillers for a bad back—and the latter for not ensuring that there were two pilots in the wheelhouse.

Two years earlier, during the panic that followed the World Trade Center bombing, the captains and crews of the Staten Island ferries played an epic role in evacuating downtown Manhattan, piloting their smoke-filled boats by radar through the harbor, the air being so saturated with dust and ash that visibility fell to near zero. On that day a fleet of ferries, tugs, Coast Guard ships, and privately-owned craft evacuated perhaps half a million people from Lower Manhattan (estimates range from 300,000 to more than a million), the largest maritime evacuation in history. A heroic day for one of Staten Island's great icons.

SAILORS' SNUG HARBOR

If you journey westward along Richmond Terrace, you'll pass by auto body shops, loading docks, chain link fences, and scraggly vacant lots. And then, just past Tysen St, a vista opens: a wide lawn and, on a slight rise, a row of five Greek Revival "temples," white, formal, graciously spaced. Originally Sailors' Snug Harbor, it is now Snug Harbor Cultural Center and Botanical Garden (*map p. 261, E1*), an umbrella organization for the performing and visual arts, environmental and educational programs. It is also one of the most beautiful places on Staten Island, and one of the best groupings of Greek Revival architecture in the nation.

Snug Harbor owes its existence to a privateer who made a fortune at sea, and to his son who spent his life (but not his fortune) ashore. The historic buildings, wrested from the grasp of high-rise developers by Staten Island preservationists, now house art galleries, theaters, and museums;

the landscaped grounds where the Staten Island Botanical
Garden has taken root remain from the days when Sailors'
Snug Harbor was a poorhouse for seafarers.

The founding of Sailors' Snug Harbor

On 1 June 1801, Robert Richard Randall, a gentleman
farmer living a couple of miles north of New York's city
limits, drew up his will. He was a bachelor, his comfortable life underwritten by the fortune he inherited from
his father. Randall's farm stretched from Broadway to
Fifth Avenue and north from Washington Square to Tenth
Street, in what today is Greenwich Village.

Little is known of Robert Richard Randall: he belonged
to the Marine Society, an elite charity for distressed ship-
masters, their widows and orphans (George Washington
had once belonged); he subscribed to the New York Society Library, from which he checked out books on history
(Gibbon's *Decline and Fall of the Roman Empire*), explora-
tion (an account of Captain Francis Smith's voyage for the
discovery of a Northwest Passage), and agriculture (John
Mills's *New and Complete System of Practical Husbandry*,
which he renewed three times).

His inherited fortune came from the sea, which for the
most part had been good to the Randall family, though
Robert's older brother, inward bound from the West
Indies, had been knocked overboard and drowned off
Sandy Hook. Randall's father, Thomas, a Scottish immi-
grant and sea captain, created the family fortune, setting

up as a merchant and ship-owner in colonial New York. Thomas excelled in the lucrative business of privateering, attacking and plundering French vessels in the Atlantic and the Caribbean with his "private" warships, which included a fourteen-gun sloop crewed by a hundred mariners. During the French and Indian War (in England called the Seven Years' War), these ships were officially empowered by the Crown and since Randall was both owner and captain during some of these raids, he got ten percent of the value of the plundered cargo.

It is a matter of debate whether Thomas Randall crossed the line between legal privateering and criminal piracy. Whatever the case, he invested his spoils wisely (mostly in real estate) and rose to the upper echelons of New York mercantile and political society, being eventually elected to the Board of Aldermen. As a prominent merchant, he was among the founders of the Chamber of Commerce. As a seaman, he designed the red-canopied barge that ferried George Washington to the city for his inauguration, serving as coxswain for the fourteen white-clad oarsmen. At the end of his life, Thomas was Master Warden of the Port of New York and of the lighthouse at Sandy Hook. He died in 1797, leaving the farm and three other rental properties in Manhattan to his son, Robert Richard.

Robert Richard Randall died a mere four years later. His will left little to his relatives, but specified annuities and gifts to servants, including gold sleeve buttons to his housekeeper and a gold watch to his faithful overseer.

Whatever remained beyond these modest gifts—and it was a great deal—Robert Randall bequeathed to endow an asylum and hospital for old, down-on-their-luck seamen. Four days after shakily scrawling his name on the document, Randall died; he was fifty-one years old.

Randall expressed his desires specifically and memorably. The asylum would be called "Sailors' Snug Harbor," and it would shelter "aged, decrepit, and worn-out sailors" (an irresistible phrase). "Snug" connoted comfort, but nautically speaking it also meant "shipshape" or "seaworthy"; this was to be a fine refuge, no niggardly poorhouse. "Decrepit" and "worn-out" spoke to the hardships of the seafaring life. Among the thirty-seven men originally accepted at the Harbor, seven were one-legged, five were "rheumatic" (arthritic), two were blind, and another nine were lame, frost-bitten, or frail.

When the will went public, collateral relatives appeared as if by spontaneous generation. Lawsuits dragged on, the final one, filed by the Anglican bishop of Nova Scotia who declared himself a deserving relative, made its way to the US Supreme Court before it was dismissed in 1831. As soon as the last lawsuit was settled, the trustees appointed by the will began to build the first of the five gracious Greek Revival buildings facing the Kill van Kull. Though Robert Richard Randall had envisioned Snug Harbor rising on his Manhattan farm, real estate values had surged during the decades while the will was contested, and the trustees relocated the Harbor to Staten

Island, preserving the Manhattan property for income. Their decision was wise, and for more than a century the rent from the Manhattan buildings proved more than ample to operate and even expand Sailors' Snug Harbor.

The Harbor opened in 1833; its five original buildings were designed by Minard Lafever, a carpenter and self-taught architect who became instrumental in introducing the Greek Revival style to New York. The grounds occupied 102 acres, and the Harbor eventually became a town unto itself, supported by surrounding farmland. The Greek Revival buildings facing the Kill served as dormitories. Separate buildings housed a bakery, kitchens, and pantries, a hospital, a morgue, a church, a chapel, and a music hall. As Barnett Shepherd points out in his meticulously researched history *Sailors' Snug Harbor: 1801–1976*, Snug Harbor offered a soft berth. The dormitories were airy and light; female employees laundered and mended the men's clothing; their meals were served in large dining rooms.

Life at Snug Harbor

The Harbor trustees were the kind of men Thomas Randall had hobbed and nobbed with—the mayor of New York, the president of the Chamber of Commerce, the chief officers of the Marine Society, and the senior ministers of the Episcopal and Presbyterian churches. They enjoyed high political and social status, but, with the exception of the members from the Marine Society, were not necessarily men whose understanding of "aged, worn-out, and decrepit sailors" was more than academic.

Simply stranding the mariners on land did not diminish their swagger or domesticate their behavior. The freedom to come and go at will resulted in junkets to neighborhood watering holes, and sometimes errant "snugs" were found drunk on the road. In 1836, three years after the Harbor opened, the trustees instituted rules that threatened expulsion for importing "ardent spirits," using obscene language, leaving without permission, or assaulting their fellows. A few years later, gatehouses and a seven-foot spiked iron fence were installed to further discourage unauthorized comings and goings. The fence, however, was hardly an insurmountable obstacle for many of the "snugs," who had spent their working lives climbing masts and swinging from rigging.

As these forays into the world beyond the fence suggest, many old salts found Harbor existence boring, even stultifying. Some of them longed to be back at sea, where at least the long stretches of boredom gave way occasionally to heart-pounding peril. One "snug," seventy-nine-year-old William Barnes published a book (1930) entitled *When Ships Were Ships and not Tin Pots*, in which he hankered for his former life. Aboard ship there was always something to look forward to—a fearsome big sea or a rollicking big night in a new port. On shore, every day was like the one that preceded it and the one that would follow.

Novelist and reporter Theodore Dreiser, always aware of the plight of the poor, well understood the restlessness undermining the soft life and wrote about it in an essay entitled "When the Sails Are Furled," collected in *The Color of a Great City* (1923). His lyrical description might well serve as an epitaph for all those worn-out seamen who spent their last days at the Harbor. Dreiser described the air of peace and serenity that enveloped the Harbor with its green lawn, classically formal architecture, and vista of the tides ebbing and flowing in the Kill van Kull. But it was a calm he contrasted to the storms of spirit and temper within all men, and especially these men who had spent their lives at sea, for whom even the inactivity of a becalmed ship was adventure compared to the comfortable tedium of Harbor life. He saw in the old and rootless sailors, shuffling about the lawns and buildings, a fierce resentment of the grinding passage of time that had worn out their bodies and robbed them of their calling and their freedom. Snug Harbor provided a material haven, he said, in a memorable closing sentence to his essay; but where on this earth, he asked, was there a "Snug Harbor for the soul?"

Thomas Melville at Snug Harbor

Thomas Melville (1830–84), the youngest brother of novelist Herman Melville, became the third governor of Snug Harbor in 1867. His tenure in office was controversial at the beginning and scandal-ridden later on.

The Harbor trustees appointed Melville reluctantly, perhaps because of his youth or because he had never joined the Marine Society. It was not because he lacked experience at sea. As a strapping sixteen-year-old, he had shipped out on a whaler and for two decades continued as an able seaman, a mate, and finally a captain. For six years he captained the clipper ship *Meteor*, rounding the Horn and crossing the Pacific. But when he applied for the cushy Snug Harbor position, he was only thirty-seven, a stranger to New York's elite merchant society. He lobbied hard, and capitalizing on his family's ties, landed the job. His handsome salary of $2000 would double as Melville received the raises he requested. The rent-free thirty-room mansion on landscaped grounds enjoyed spectacular water views. Business dealings with the Harbor trustees offered entrée to an inner circle of New York society.

On the other hand, the stress level was high. As captain of the *Meteor*, Melville's word had been law and his authority complete. But as governor of Snug Harbor he oversaw hundreds of cantankerous old mariners who were almost always hostile to authority. He became increasingly rigid as a disciplinarian, setting down rules requiring unpaid work from able-bodied inmates (though he eventually recanted and paid the old salts fifteen cents a day), wielding the tobacco ration as a threat and requiring newcomers to pledge quiet, orderly behavior, church attendance, and abstention from alcohol. To assure compliance, he appointed monitors to spy on their fellows.

The sailors grumbled about the meals, accused Melville of brutality, and asserted that the trustees and officers were squandering the Harbor's income. In 1872, a former clerk charged Melville with appropriating the Harbor's chickens, bread, and milk for his own family. Melville denied it all, and through a combination of arm-twisting and cajolery continued in the good graces of the trustees, though the volume of the complaints suggests that they had substance.

Privately, Thomas Melville was generous and supportive, the most pleasant man in a difficult family. He liked the role of genial host, and at his trustees' dinners would invite fifty or so of his gentlemen friends. Occasionally even Herman Melville—living in New York, increasingly depressed and reclusive as the critics continued to excoriate his new work—would join these gatherings. He called Staten Island "Tom's Paradise."

The stress took a toll on Thomas Melville's health. On 5 March 1884, he came home from work feeling well but began to have difficulty breathing. In three hours he was dead. The *Staten Island Gazette and Sentinel* opined, "Like most really strong men, he was one of the tenderest. [...] All who knew him respected him, all who knew him intimately loved him, loved him the more the better they knew him." Perhaps the writer was simply speaking well of the dead, but as the pallbearers carried his body out of the gate for burial at the Moravian Cemetery, the old sailors stood with bared heads, at least a few moved to tears.

Snug Harbor today

After World War II, the income from the Manhattan real estate decreased, as did the pool of indigent sailors: at its peak, the Harbor had a thousand "snugs" but by the mid-twentieth century many sailors were family men with pensions, social security benefits, and zero desire to live in an institution. In 1976, the courts allowed the Trustees to move the Harbor and its remaining 111 retirees to a new facility at Sea Level, North Carolina, and the 130 acres of vacant Staten Island waterfront property suddenly took on the appearance of the promised land for eager developers.

After years of negotiations, lawsuits, and politicking, the City of New York bought 83.3 acres and converted Snug Harbor to the present cultural center, retaining the landmarked buildings and gradually rehabilitating them. Most of the cultural institutions there today have no particular connection to the history of the Harbor, but simply take advantage of the site and its architecture. However, the Noble Maritime Center, which honors the life and work of John Alexander Noble (*see below*), lies close to the spirit of the old sailors' retreat.

John A. Noble, salvage artist

Maritime artist John Alexander Noble (1913–85) came by his visual gifts and his unconventional character genetically. He was born in Paris, where his father, John "Wichita Bill" Noble, was living a bohemian existence subsidized by his own wealthy father. As a young Kansan painter, Wichita Bill had specialized in cowboy scenes and the occasional barroom nude (one of which provoked prohibitionist Carrie Nation to fling a billiard ball at the offending canvas). Wichita Bill couldn't leave Kansas soon enough, but once in Paris he flaunted his frontier identity, donning a white sombrero and spinning tall tales of prairie hardships. He married and began painting the coast of Brittany, becoming as his son said, "a sort of mystic painter of the sea." Romantic, eccentric, and eventually alcoholic, he died in Bellevue Hospital of an overdose of paraldehyde, a sedative given to quiet the DTs.

When he was six, John Noble *fils* arrived in New York with his parents and his little brother Towanda (named for a Kansas prairie town). He spent his childhood summers at Provincetown on Cape Cod, where his father belonged to a colony of painters, poets, and playwrights. Though John Noble received a privileged education, attending the Friends Seminary in New York and studying in Grenoble and at the National Academy of Design, he worked for years on ships and in marine salvage, spending time with "factory people, industrial people, the immigrants, the sons of immigrants," who in his opinion gave the city its vitality. When he was fifteen, working on a schooner on the Kill van Kull, he noticed the Port Johnston coal docks on the Jersey side of the kill, by then a graveyard of wooden sailing vessels. In those obsolescent, discarded, and decaying craft, Noble saw his mission. For the rest of his life his eye was drawn by ships whose better days had come and gone.

Erin Urban, whose beautifully illustrated biography *Hulls and Hulks in the Tide of Time* is the definitive work on Noble, quotes this 1933 note from Noble to his mother—a statement of his life's work and an indication that in addition to his visual talents he was also gifted as writer:

> So many times it has been my fate to see the strange ends and beginnings of things on the water. It makes me uneasy. I don't have the same fate on land, which hides its color from me. But on the water, where there are no or just a couple of people, destiny crawls, and only I see it. I wish I didn't.

He documented the decline of sailing ships, the coming of steamships, and then the rise of the diesel-driven container ships and tankers that today make up much of the traffic through the kills.

His weathered skin marked him as an outdoorsman; his burly body and bristling hair implied energy and substance. His style was rough: he smoked and drank a lot in the bars where seamen gathered. In 1974, on what would have been Wichita Bill's hundredth birthday, John spent the evening in two of his favorite bars, buying drinks in honor of his father, running up a tab reckoned at $70.

His work in marine salvage led him to his own projects: he built a floating "houseboat" studio from parts of ships he'd retrieved from the boneyards and docked it at Port Johnston. When his family had grown to include two sons, he bought a house on Richmond Terrace close to the ferry station, where he could look out over the harbor. Given Noble's skills in carpentry, it was a small step for him to improve the house by cutting portholes in walls and the living room floor.

He painted in oils; he made lithographs; he drew in charcoal, but his subject was almost always the passing of the age of sail, the loss of the great wooden ships to a new technology. And yet as he said in a memoir, he was "just as interested in drawing the building of a great modern tanker, the working of a modern dredge, as…in the shifting of topsails…anywhere men work or build on the water is of interest to me."

John Noble died in 1985. Many of his paintings and lithographs, the Noble Maritime Collection, are hung in a beautifully restored former dormitory building of Sailors' Snug Harbor, a perfect match of setting and content. The centerpiece of the permanent exhibition is Noble's houseboat studio, which was taken apart, restored, and reassembled. You can peer inside the cabin and admire Noble's skill as a carpenter, his ingenuity as a designer, and the beauty of the materials from which the old ships were made. In addition to Noble's own paintings, drawings, and prints, there is a recreation of Wichita Bill's studio and an assemblage of ship models—from the small and crude to the impressive and intricate—as well as an exhibit of what the building looked like before volunteers reconstructed it. The reconstruction gives you an idea of the architectural elegance in which the "snugs" spent their declining years. And also of the amount of work necessary to return the building to its earlier beauty.

THE OYSTERS OF STATEN ISLAND

Six hundred years ago, oyster shells paved the floor of New York harbor. Their beds covered 350 square miles, stretching north up the Hudson and east through Hell Gate and Long Island Sound, wrapping around the Brooklyn coastline to Jamaica Bay and the Rockaway Peninsula, reaching south along the New Jersey shore to Keyport, and girding the harbor reefs of Ellis Island and Liberty Island (known in colonial days as Little and Big Oyster Island).

The oysters were big, sometimes a foot across. But then the entire harbor so teemed with life that the first European explorers thought they had sailed into a new Eden: the striped bass were so thick in the water, they said, that you could almost pull them out by hand and the lobsters were six feet long. Everything in this new world was plentiful, supersized—perhaps a token of the mega-city to come.

According to Mark Kurlansky's entertaining and informative *The Big Oyster: History on the Half Shell*, Staten Island had some of the best oyster beds—in Raritan Bay, in the Arthur Kill and the Kill van Kull, at Prince's Bay, and Great Kills. For the Lenape, oysters were a dietary staple, and until pollution closed the beds, oysters were a mainstay of Staten Island's economy. Small coastal towns—Prince's Bay, Tottenville—existed on oystering. In the opening years of the nineteenth century, oystering and its ancillary trades employed a thousand or more people in a population of about 67,000. A few families got rich pulling the delectable bivalves out of the water or hiring others to do it for them. Others, including the African Americans in Sandy Ground, made decent livings.

The Lenape lacked tools to pry apart the shells, but still managed to consume great quantities, presumably opening them with the aid of fire. Their middens (mounds of discarded shells) turned up all over New York City, from the Rockaways in Queens to Tottenville at the southwest tip of Staten Island. The Lenape drilled clam shells for wampum—money—and they buried some of their dead, both human and canine, beneath blankets of oyster shells. Probably to their eventual sorrow, they shared their oystering skills with the Dutch, who arrived in the seventeenth century.

Harvesting oysters was hard work, as the colonists learned. European oysters lay in shallow beds accessible to raking, but here in America they lay deeper. The oysterman rowed his skiff out to the beds and, standing in the boat, he lowered 15- or 20-foot clawed tongs into the water, worked the long handles back and forth to scoop up the oysters, lifted the catch to the surface hand-over-hand, and swung the oysters into the boat to be culled, rowed ashore, and shucked. The work was back-breaking at best and dangerous in rough water, but its very difficulty ensured that the oyster beds would not be over-fished, at least for a while.

The boats for tonging, called Staten Island skiffs or Yankee skiffs, were beautiful: elegantly curved and low to the water but broad enough to be stable while the catch was lifted. Some local oystermen owned sloops for carrying the oysters to market in Manhattan, where the wholesalers set up shop. The trade had the simplicity and immediacy of a cottage industry, its tools reaching the status of art objects. An illustration in *Ballou's Pictorial Drawing-Room Companion* in 1855 (which inspired a painting owned by the Staten Island Historical Society) shows two black oystermen standing in a skiff, the ruddy cliffs of Prince's Bay and its lighthouse in the background.

But by the opening decades of the nineteenth century, even though harvesting was laborious, the natural Staten Island beds were showing signs of exhaustion. Fortunately, technology enabled oystermen to replenish the beds "from seed," transplanting newly-spawned oysters from more fertile areas and replanting them to fatten close to their markets. Staten Islanders first culled seed from the Arthur Kill and the waters around Long Island; later they journeyed to the Chesapeake Bay, the center of the American industry. Seeding slowed the decline of the oyster beds and at the end of the nineteenth century Staten Island waters still produced more than 200,000 bushels of oysters annually. Seeding also brought Chesapeake Bay oystermen north, where they helped prepare the beds, raking over the old shells and spreading the seed oysters evenly over the bay floor so that they would grow larger, like trees optimally spaced in open fields.

Meanwhile, in New York City more people were consuming more of everything including oysters. In 1898, when the five boroughs were consolidated, every day as many as one million oysters slid down the throats of the city's 2.5 million citizens. The poor bought them for a penny apiece at street stands or in basement dives; the wealthy impaled them on silver forks in fine restaurants. At a time when appetites were as swollen as the ambitions of the robber barons, a dozen oysters (four dozen for "Diamond Jim" Brady) served as a mere warm-up to the soup, fish, roasts, game, vegetables, salads, sherbet, and desserts that would follow in the normal course of a dinner. One gourmand claimed to have devoured 120 raw oysters at a sitting. (This seems remarkable, but on the other hand, the 2012 winner of the Nathan's Hot Dog Eating Contest at Coney Island downed sixty-eight hot dogs and buns in ten minutes.)

But while seeding kept the beds alive, technological advances in shipbuilding soon threatened the oysters with extinction. First came schooners, bigger than the sloops, able to carry larger cargoes of oysters ashore. Then came dredges, whose iron bars, dragged across the harbor floor, scooped up hundreds of oysters at a single pass but at the same time silted the water, scarred the harbor floor, and degraded the environment. Dredging was bad enough when done under sail, but with the advent of steam engines it became brutally efficient.

Pollution would finish off what over-harvesting had begun. New Yorkers had been treating the harbor as their own public and private sewer for almost 200 years, and by the end of the nineteenth century by-products from dye factories, fertilizer companies, chemical plants, and petroleum storage dumps, many of them clustered around the kills, when added to the raw sewage daily poured into the rivers, turned the waters around the city into a foul broth. Several cases of cholera were traced to polluted oysters. Gradually the city health department began closing the beds: Staten Island's, in 1916, were the first to go.

SANDY GROUND: A FREE AFRICAN AMERICAN COMMUNITY

Sandy Ground, between Tottenville and Woodrow (*map p. 262, B5*), was one of the first free African American communities in what is now New York. Its fortunes rose and fell with the oyster business, and nowadays there is little to see: a couple of nineteenth-century houses, much altered but preserved by landmarking; a small church with its graveyard behind a chain link fence; and a museum. And yet Sandy Ground has been commemorated in print, its cemetery enrolled in the National Register of Historic

Places, its church landmarked, and its local history memorialized by the Sandy Ground Historical Society, which maintains the community archives and mounts exhibits.

There never *was* much to see, but from the years before the Civil War until the oyster beds were closed, Sandy Ground thrived—mostly segregated, mostly poor, but independent and proud. Through time the village had several names: Bogardus Corners, Harrisville, Little Africa. The first settlers were whites of European origin and the place eventually took the name Sandy Ground from the loamy soil. The first black landowner was John Jackson, who in 1828 bought two and a half acres nearby; he seems to have earned his living captaining a ferry up the Arthur Kill to New York. Subsequent black residents arrived from Manhattan, fleeing the German and Irish immigrants who had begun crowding into the slums in the 1840s. Most of Sandy Ground's arrivals in the 1850s and 1860s came from New York City or State and continued to farm the sandy soil, which was hospitable to strawberries.

The oystermen came later, mainly from the Chesapeake Bay area in Maryland and Virginia. New York had abolished slavery in 1827, but Maryland and Virginia remained slave states, with Maryland having the highest population of free blacks in the nation. White Marylanders, believing that free blacks threatened the institution of slavery, passed restrictive laws prohibiting free black oystermen from owning ships or captaining those owned by whites unless a white man was on board. Free blacks could not work as carpenters, own carts or drays, or sell produce on the open market; if a free black left the state for more than thirty days, he or she would fall back into slavery.

For obvious reasons, some of the oystermen who sailed north with seed oysters to replenish Staten Island's beds decided to stay, settling in Sandy Ground. Staten Island historian Barnett Shepherd considers the actual founding of the community to date from the founding of the African Methodist Episcopal Zion Church in 1850. By the 1860s and 1870s many of the new arrivals from the South had put down roots and prospered, both on water and on land: some of the men became basket makers, woodworkers, or blacksmiths, forging oyster tongs and rakes, repairing ships. The women worked as domestics for white families in the adjacent towns. Several of the oystermen owned skiffs or sloops, and many families owned their homes.

Toward the end of the nineteenth century, large New York wholesalers began to dominate the market. The newly formed companies moved into Staten Island waters and lobbied successfully for laws that gave them legal rights to the beds, which formerly were allocated by custom: an oysterman could work a bed as long as he staked it out and used it. In old pictures of oystermen at work you can see the stakes marking individual beds sticking up through the water. The companies' powerful boats and dredgers left the local oystermen at a disadvantage, eventually squeezing them out of the industry.

The closing of the oyster beds was a tragedy for Sandy Ground. African American men who had worked on the water could only find less lucrative and less satisfying jobs as school janitors, garbage men, or porters; some found factory work across the kill in New Jersey. Children grew up and moved to places with better opportunities. By the 1950s, the town was a shadow of its former self.

The construction boom following the opening of the Verrazano-Narrows Bridge delivered the final blow. Frederick Law Olmsted in 1871, with startling prescience, had inveighed against developers who built houses because of the beauty of the land and in the process destroyed that very beauty: Sandy Ground is just one community that has suffered from overbuilding. In 1963, many of the houses were burned in a brush fire, and most of those remaining have been bulldozed. Look-alike models now stand shoulder to shoulder along the old streets named for early Staten Island families (Winant Avenue) or for destinations (Woodrow Road) or for geographical features (Clay Pit Road). The new houses are mostly well-kept and there is pride of place; but the old Sandy Ground houses were built not in batches, but one by one, when people needed or could afford them. Wood-frame, shingle-sided or clapboarded, they were constructed by owners skilled in carpentry or by builders from nearby Pleasant Plains or Tottenville. Today only about a half dozen still stand, mainly because of the determination of their owners, often descendants of the earlier Sandy Grounders, as does the A.M.E. Zion Church (584

Bloomingdale Rd.; map p. 262, A5–B5), once the center of the community.

Two voices from Sandy Ground:
George H. Hunter and Lois A.H. Mosley

On several occasions in the 1940s and 1950s, writer Joseph Mitchell visited George H. Hunter (1869–1967) at his home in Sandy Ground. Mitchell's specialty was interviews. A good listener, he wrote down what people said, catching their turns of phrase, letting them speak in their own voices. Mitchell's story, "Mr. Hunter's Grave," appeared in *The New Yorker* in September 1956 and, republished in *The Bottom of the Harbor*, has become a classic.

Lois A.H. Mosley, born a couple of generations later (1927–2008), published her own recollections as *Sandy Ground Memories* in 2003. In shaping the book she was helped by historian Barnett Shepherd, but it is Mrs. Mosley's own voice that comes through—clear, frank, humorous, understated, accepting.

Mr. Hunter and Mrs. Mosley are part of the reason the place continues to live in memory. Mr. Hunter would not have liked the Sandy Ground of 2012. Even back in 1956, he distrusted what it had become. In the old days, he said, people took care of things, kept up their houses, gardened, canned, painted, built what they needed. They made things that lasted. But by the 1950s, people were not so neighborly, no longer sat on their porches but inside watching television. They bought refrigerators and cars, even sometimes on the installment plan, which to Hunter spelled trouble.

George H. Hunter had prospered through hard work and ability. He started his work life as a farm laborer; as a teenager he cooked on a fishing boat, and then carried and laid bricks. He became skillful at arching and vaulting, and since rural Staten Island lacked public sewers, he borrowed money to start his own business constructing and cleaning cesspools. He thrived, lived in a good-sized house, became a pillar of the A.M.E. Zion Church, and in his old age, insofar as he was able, he kept up the cemetery, though he viewed gravestones as the last vestige of human vanity: even stones do not last forever; only the spirit endures. Mr. Hunter himself lasted a long time, returning to his maker when he was close to 100 years old.

Lois Mosley, born in Sandy Ground, remained there until 1957, when poverty forced her to move to public housing in Port Richmond. She grew up during the Depression, when a quarter was "heavy money." Her father, gifted as a musician and athlete, made his living delivering coal and ice in New Jersey; when she was twelve he abandoned the family, leaving her mother to raise four children. Her ancestors had done well in the oyster business; her grandfather and great-uncle had owned sloops, but when the oystering days ended, they had turned to farming.

Mrs. Mosley speaks of her childhood with great warmth—her family was poor but resourceful. They had a coal stove for heat and an ice box for cooling things. The coal man, ice man, fish man, rag man, and knife-and-scissor man made rounds. Mrs. Mosley considered George H. Hunter one of the town's wealthier people, especially since he had an indoor toilet (but, after all, his business was cesspools).

She endured racial prejudice. Two junior high school teachers belittled her and the other black children. Competition with white oystermen caused problems for black oystermen. The black taxi owner was abducted and beaten, she thought by white competitors. She never became as financially comfortable as Mr. Hunter, but her life tracked upward. After high school, she worked as a cook; she earned an associate's degree in dietetics and eventually, when she was forty-six, a bachelor's degree. She worked in hospitals and schools; she taught cooking at the A.M.E. Zion Church. She raised six children, sometimes holding down three jobs to support them, earning the affection and loyalty of many people both black and white. Her voice is softer than Mr. Hunter's, modulated by humor and forgiveness.

What was it about the place that they revered? For Mr. Hunter, it was the values of hard work, religious faith, decency, and kindness; it was also the independence that Sandy Ground sometimes afforded African Americans, for example the oystermen who owned their boats. For Mrs. Mosley, it was the love and support of a community of people like herself, who called it home.

THE LIGHTHOUSES OF STATEN ISLAND

Staten Island lies just west of the main channel leading into the port of New York, a channel hazardous with shifting sandbars and reefs, some barely submerged. From an early date pilots were needed to guide ships in and out of the port, and a system of organized pilotage came into existence as early as 1837. The earliest lighthouse in Staten Island waters dates from a year later.

Thanks in part to the work of volunteers, Staten Island now has as many historic lighthouses as the other boroughs put together, not even counting those in surrounding waters that belong to New Jersey. There are three on high ground—the Staten Island Range Light, the New Dorp Light, and the Prince's Bay Light—and two on the shoreline—the Fort Wadsworth and Elm Tree Lights. Offshore are the West Bank Lighthouse (east of South Beach), the Robbins Reef Lighthouse (at the mouth of the Kill van Kull), and the Great Beds Light (at the mouth of the Arthur Kill), the last two belonging to New Jersey. The Old Orchard Shoal Light (1893) stood in Raritan Bay about three miles east of Great Kills Park until 2012, when the 25-foot waves of Hurricane Sandy tore it from its foundation and sent it to the bottom of the harbor where it lies under 17 feet of water. It may be possible to retrieve and perhaps reassemble it on the site of the former US Lighthouse Service's General Depot in St. George.

THE LIGHTHOUSE DEPOT

In its heyday, the US Lighthouse Depot in St. George received, uncrated, inspected, and reshipped the imported Fresnel lenses for all of the lighthouses in the district, which stretched from Sandy Hook to the Massachusetts border; underground vaults stored fuel for the lighthouses; machine shops and foundries fabricated buoys, anchors, and the structural parts for the buildings of the service. The Depot, just south of the St. George Ferry terminal, was taken over by the US Coast Guard in 1939 but closed in 1965 when its navigational aids were automated. Presently owned by the City of New York, the former Depot has been chosen as the site of the National Lighthouse Museum, which is presently trying to fund the project. Several of the piers are now used as a maintenance facility for the Staten Island Ferry; a mixed-use development with stores and condominiums has been proposed for part of the site.

Katherine Walker and the Robbins Reef Lighthouse

The Coast Guard cutter *Katherine Walker* ranges New York harbor servicing buoys, searching, rescuing, protecting, and occasionally breaking ice. So it's entirely fitting that this workhorse of a ship should bear the name of a small, slight woman, a lighthouse keeper of Teutonic determination and significant upper body strength. For thirty-three years she manned the light at Robbins Reef, mostly by herself. Though the lighthouse belongs to New Jersey, Katherine Walker identified with Staten Island and is buried there.

Kate Walker (1848–1931), née Gortler, widowed and with a young son, emigrated from Germany hoping for opportunity. Waiting tables in a Sandy Hook boarding house, she met her second husband, John Walker, the assistant keeper of the Sandy Hook lighthouse. When Walker was transferred to the Robbins Reef Lighthouse, Katherine's life constricted—no more vegetable and flower gardens, no more keeper's house, no more land. The Robbins Reef Lighthouse (*map p. 6, C1*) is a four-story metal spark-plug lighthouse standing gamely on a desolate offshore foundation hardly bigger than the base of the tower itself. The living quarters, now gone, wrapped around the tower's base like a life buoy around a drowning swimmer. The tower, painted brown and white, rose 46 feet above the water, with full views of the harbor.

The tower marks a reef where in Dutch colonial days seals hauled up on the rocks (*robyn* is Dutch for "seal"). At first Katherine refused to unpack her trunks, unwilling to think of this lonely place as home. Eventually she settled in, had another child, and adjusted to life on a granite pile. Later she would prefer its solitude to the push and shove of New York.

Then, John Walker got pneumonia; as he was rowed ashore to the hospital, he turned to his wife and said,

"Mind the light, Kate." He died in the hospital in 1890. A substitute came so that she could attend his funeral, but she was back on the job before the sun set. She took his final words to heart. For thirty-three years. Every morning she stood at the porthole and looked towards his grave. Whether the hills of Staten Island were brown, or green, or white with snow, she always heard a message from her husband, just three words: "Mind the light."

The keeper's duties were demanding, especially for a woman who was four feet ten inches tall and weighed about a hundred pounds. Daily she polished the lamp and its reflectors, washed the windows, trimmed the wick, and filled the reservoir with oil. At night, every three hours or so, she wound the weights that kept the beacon rotating; in between she polished the brass fittings and kept house. When fog masked the light, she descended into the deep basement and started the steam engine that sounded the horn at three-second intervals. When the engine broke down, she climbed the metal ladder to the tower and clanged on a huge bell.

The lighthouse foundation, a granite caisson, was too small to dock a boat, so the dinghy hung by chains from davits outside the kitchen. Walker used the dinghy to row her children to school on Staten Island, about a mile away. By her own count, she also rowed out to save some fifty people, mostly fishermen, who washed up on the reef. She also rescued a dog, comforting it with warm coffee for which, she thought, the creature expressed gratitude.

In 1894, after working at laborer's wages for several years, she was appointed lighthouse keeper, but only after two men had turned down the job as unbearably lonely. Her son helped, though he moved ashore after his marriage. She retired and moved to Staten Island in 1919 (she was seventy-three), still within sight of the light. The Coast Guard took it over in 1939 and staffed it with a team of three keepers to do the work Katherine had managed alone; in 1966, the light was automated and today it is run by solar power. In 2009, it was declared surplus and was granted to the Noble Maritime Collection (*see p. 73*), which hopes to turn the lower level into a museum.

Elm Tree Lighthouse

In the eighteenth century, Staten Island sailors navigated using an elm tree at the site of present Miller Field (*map p. 261, E4*) as a point of reference. By 1856, a beacon on a tower had replaced the tree, the light functioning as the front (lower) range light for the New Dorp Lighthouse sited about two miles inland on a hill. (Range lights, paired beacons separated by distance and elevation, are positioned to guide vessels entering a difficult channel; when viewed from the passing ship, the lights appear to be aligned vertically, i.e. "on range," only when the ship is on the correct course.) The present lighthouse, a drab octagonal concrete tower, was built in 1939 by the US Coast Guard to replace the wooden tower. In 1964, channel markers replaced both the Elm Tree and New Dorp range lights.

New Dorp (Swash Channel Range Rear) Light

The New Dorp Light (1856), situated on a hillside above the Moravian Cemetery (*map p. 261, D4*), looks like, and is, a house with a tower poking out of the roof. Originally it served as the rear light of the Swash Channel Range Light, indicating safe passage through one of the natural channels in the sandbar across the harbor mouth. When built, the lantern room at 192 feet above sea level offered a view across the cemetery as far as Sandy Hook in New Jersey. The government's right-of-way to the lighthouse was a narrow path through the surrounding forest, not wide enough for a horse and wagon, but until the cemetery trustees and the Lighthouse Board quarreled over land rights, the trustees allowed keepers to haul supplies with a horse and wagon up the hill on the cemetery road. In 1878, the trustees prohibited use of their road, and for eleven years the lighthouse keeper had to carry everything on foot or on horseback. Eventually the government ceded its right-of-way to the cemetery in exchange for access to their road. In 1964, the light was deactivated and ten years later the abandoned building was bought at auction by a private citizen who restored it board by board, nail by nail.

West Bank Light

The West Bank Lighthouse, which serves as the front light for the Staten Island Range Light, is a metal spark-plug tower built in 1901. Located offshore, east of Great Kills Park (*map p. 6, C3*), it marks the Ambrose Channel, the main entrance to New York Harbor, completed in 1914. The lighthouse was automated in 1980, converted to solar power in 1998, declared excess by the Coast Guard in 2007, and is now privately owned. The first keeper was the legendary Ed Burdge, who spent thirty-four years manning different lights around the Lower Bay, a quiet man whose celebrity outside the lighthouse service arose largely from a colorful interview in *American Magazine* in 1924. Burdge seems to have been born for the solitary life; physically courageous and independent, he enjoyed disabusing landlubbers of any romantic notions they might harbor about the quiet life of a lighthouse keeper:

> I met a lady once who was all filled up with what she called the romance of the lighthouse…A lighthouse is about the noisiest place in the world…Forty or sixty tons of water, driven by a fifty-mile gale, racing in with the tide and slamming against a solid tower of stone and iron makes it about as quiet as when two railroad trains butt each other head on. Down at the floor level, there is a gas engine pounding away, with the exhaust exploding outside, the iron plates in the tower groaning, the fog siren screaming, and the bell ringing, and up in the light a stream of kerosene burning under a hundred pound pressure, and roaring louder than [a] gale. Nice, romantic spot—so quiet that the keeper can scarcely hear the whistles of steamers and tugs in the channel.

The Staten Island Range Light

The Staten Island Range Light, also known as the Ambrose Channel Range Light on Richmond Hill (*Edinboro Rd.; map p. 263, D4*) is surely the most dramatic of the Island's towers and the most beautiful. It is five miles away from the West Bank Light and sited 141 feet higher. First lit in 1912, when the uncompleted Ambrose Channel was already in use, it was powered by a kerosene vapor lamp, electrified in 1939, and eventually automated; it still serves as an active aid to navigation. The tower is built of pale yellow brick and sits on a limestone base. The nearby keeper's house (now privately owned), built of the same brick, is elegant by any standards, with a parlor, three bedrooms, and a kitchen and pantry; when the tower was manned, an electric bell connected the keeper with his household. In 1992, Joe Esposito—a neighborhood lighthouse aficionado with skills as an electrician, carpenter, and mason—began tending the place without pay, doing everything from mowing the lawn to showing visitors around; medical problems forced him to retire in 2001, but the Coast Guard issued him a certificate of merit commending him for his volunteer service.

FRANK LLOYD WRIGHT ON STATEN ISLAND

Frank Lloyd Wright endowed New York City with two buildings: the Guggenheim Museum, which is world famous; and "Crimson Beech," which is not. "Crimson

Beech," named for the copper beech tree that formerly grew in the yard of 48 Manor Court, just southwest of the Range Light, was commissioned by William and Catherine Cass, who had followed Wright's work and seen him in a TV interview.

Like Wright's other Usonian houses (Wright used "Usonian" instead of "American" to suggest a New World mode of design), "Crimson Beech" is pre-fabricated (Pre-Fab No. 1, 1956) to offer beautiful and efficient design at a moderate price. (In practice, Wright's Usonian houses cost about the same as those built with traditional construction techniques.) The house lies flat against the hillside, one story in front but two in back where the slope falls away. The overhanging roof and continuous windows—narrow clerestory facing the street to provide privacy, more expansive in the back to take in the view—are also features of other Usonian houses, as are the carport and the L-configuration, which allows a bigger house on a small building lot. The components were fabricated in Wisconsin, then trucked in and assembled on site; the house itself plus shipping cost $20,000, well within the Casses' budget of $35,000 in 1958, but local contractors tacked on another $35,000. The shell of the house was assembled in only five days; the finishing took four months. The original copper beech tree that gave the house its name is gone, but the brick gatepost with its built-in mailbox, designed by Wright, remains.

NATURAL STATEN ISLAND

Staten Island Naturalists—Henry David Thoreau—Frederick Law Olmsted—The Greenbelt—Freshkills Park

Staten Island was once very beautiful and, in places, it still is. Early visitors unanimously admired the Island's beauty, its fertility, its expansiveness. Giovanni da Verrazano, who anchored in the Narrows in 1524, looked ashore and saw (as the historical sign at Fort Wadsworth translates his description) "a pleasant place beneath steep little hills…and from among those hills a mighty deep-mouthed river [that] ran outward to the sea." Though he regretted leaving, the Florentine navigator was driven out to sea by a sudden squall and never went ashore.

Eighty-five years later Henry Hudson did make landfall, and also reported a marvelously fertile land whose air smelled sweet and whose meadows were filled with grasses, flowers, and imposing trees; the surrounding seas teemed with salmon, mullets, and rays so large it took several men to haul them aboard. English-born Daniel Denton (c.1626–1703), trying to drum up interest in real estate he hoped to develop, spoke of fields bedecked with roses and other wild flowers. Staten Island was a new Eden.

If you believe George William Curtis, the nineteenth-century essayist, educator, and second-string Transcendentalist, the Island's landscape was indeed the handiwork of God, who could have made a more beautiful place, but chose not to.

What remains of that landscape—the Greenbelt (*see p. 110*) and other parks and protected land—will make you understand what Curtis had in mind, but this extensive swathe of green has resulted not from divine favor but from the protracted struggles of modern preservationists and environmentalists, preceded by a remarkable group of amateur and professional scientists who thrived between about 1880 and 1930.

STATEN ISLAND NATURALISTS

In the nineteenth century, when science (mostly observational and descriptive rather than experimental) was attracting interest both as a hobby and as a profession, Staten Island nurtured a fine brood of naturalists, who described its geology, flora, and fauna. Some of them founded scientific institutions that have achieved local and national reputations. Many contributed to the museums that were burgeoning in the second half of the nineteenth century: the American Museum of Natural History (1869), the Staten Island Institute of Arts & Sciences (1881), and the New York Botanical Garden (1891). As a group, these naturalists were adventurous, traveling widely and experiencing primitive conditions in remote places. Some became expert in small corners of specialized fields: cicadas, beetles, mollusk shells, fossil plants. Two off-islanders who lived

here for a while, Frederick Law Olmsted and Henry David
Thoreau, influenced future generations as much with their
philosophies of nature and society as with their local observations.

Foremost among the local naturalists, perhaps, was **Nathaniel Lord Britton** (1859–1934), who taught geology
and botany at what is now Columbia University and with
his wife co-founded the New York Botanical Garden, in
a wooded area of the Bronx formerly owned by the to-
bacco-growing Lorillard family. Among Britton's volumi-
nous publications were studies of Staten Island's flora, but
also works on the plant life of New Jersey, New England,
North America, and the Caribbean, where he wintered
when New York got too cold. His four-volume study *The
Cactaceae* crowned eighteen years of fieldwork and the
subsequent writing and rewriting. Britton's parents had
envisioned a religious career for him, and a photo taken in
his maturity depicts him as an ascetic-looking man (with a
comb-over clinging to his skull), someone who might well
have gravitated to the church. Unfortunately for his parents' hopes, a passion for botany seized him early, and he
spent his life looking earthward rather than heavenward.
An admirable organizer and fundraiser, Britton encour-
aged financial support for the Botanical Garden by naming plants for wealthy donors. Britton was descended from
an old Staten Island family and the Britton ancestral home
has been preserved at Historic Richmond Town (*see p. 47*).

At a time when women had few opportunities as scientists, his wife **Elizabeth Britton** (née Elizabeth Gertrude Knight; 1858–1934) was as energetic and productive as her husband, and as adventurous. Her specialty was bryology, the study of mosses, on which she published 170 of her 346 scientific papers. A passionate field worker, she collected in the Adirondacks and the Appalachian Mountains, Puerto Rico, Cuba, and Jamaica. She became honorary curator at the New York Botanical Garden and oversaw the work of doctoral students at Columbia College though she had no advanced academic degree; she was the only woman nominated as a charter member of the American Botanical Society. As an ecologist, she worked for the preservation of native plants and was a founder of the American Wildflower Preservation Society.

Louis Pope Gratacap (1851–1917), a career scientist with the American Museum of Natural History, wrote a classic work on New York geology, studied the flora and fauna of Central Park, published books on theological subjects, and authored science fiction novels in his spare time. A bachelor, he lived on the family homestead in West Brighton on the North Shore and spent the three-hour daily commute to the Museum on Manhattan's Upper West Side industriously reading.

Charles Arthur Hollick (1857–1933) made a career of paleobotany, collecting plant fossils in Wyoming and

Colorado, and teaching drawing to students of geology and paleontology. As Sanitary Engineer for the Board of Health of New Brighton, he established a sewerage system on Staten Island and worked to abate the air pollution from New Jersey factories; in 1903, he spent four months in Canada and Alaska traveling a thousand miles down the Yukon River, from Dawson City to Anvik, for the US Geological Survey. During Hollick's last collecting expedition, to Cuba when he was seventy-six, he logged another thousand miles on foot, horseback, and in primitive conveyances—which may have been hazardous to his health as he died three months later.

William T. Davis, if not as famous professionally as the other four, was perhaps the most important to Staten Island, where he is remembered as much for his activism as a conservationist and preservationist as for his scientific discoveries. A separate section is devoted to him below.

One of Davis's protégés was **Alanson Buck Skinner** (1886–1925), who in his short life became an outstanding ethnologist. Skinner came to Staten Island as a small child, and Davis took him under his wing, leading him and other interested boys on "tramps," to study the Island's natural history and forage for arrowheads. Skinner succeeded in finding arrowheads and at the same time discovered his life's work. While still in high school he trekked out to Long Island with anthropologists from the American Museum of Natural History to study ancient Shinnecock shell middens. After graduation he joined the staff of the AMNH and began exploring further afield, leading a group to remote Hudson Bay when he was only twenty-two, traveling hundreds of miles by eighteen-foot canoe. Two years later, he and two companions paddled through the Everglades to areas never before visited by white men, gathering artifacts from the few Seminoles who remained there. Skinner studied the Sauk, the Potawatomi, the Iowa, the Cree, the Plains Ojibway, the Saulteaux, the Eastern-Dakota, and even the Bribri of Costa Rica, but his special interest became the Menomini of Wisconsin, who adopted him into the tribe, calling him "Little Weasel." He married a Wyandotte woman and was proud that his wife and daughter had Native American blood. Sympathetic to the culture and the problems of the peoples he studied, he was trusted and admired. In addition to his work as an ethnologist, Skinner wrote a couple of stories for *Weird Tales*, a pulp fiction magazine. He died while collecting in North Dakota; the Ford touring car in which he was riding, driven by Amos Oneroad, Skinner's friend and co-worker, slid off a muddy road and down an embankment near Tokio, North Dakota, throwing him out and killing him.

William T. Davis

William Thompson Davis (1862–1945) was born to be a naturalist. According to his biographer Mabel Abbott, he started early, jotting down scientific observations in a journal whose first entry noted twenty ants on a piece of bread. When he was twenty-two, he had already planned out his future, pointing out that he had saved $1,300 toward his calling as a "tramp." Davis had no intention of becoming a career vagrant: he planned to spend his life "tramping" around Staten Island observing nature. He did so in sunshine and rain, day and night, winter and summer, from childhood into old age.

He published some five hundred scientific papers, among them "Whirligig Beetles Taking a Sun-Bath," "Intelligence Shown by Caterpillars in Placing Their Cocoons," and "Shooting Insects with a Bean Shooter." He founded the organization that would become the Staten Island Institute of Arts & Sciences. He and Charles W. Leng, a fellow beetle enthusiast, researched and co-wrote the still-definitive history of Staten Island. He copied gravestone inscriptions, collected folklore, studied place names, and for a time served as the president of the Staten Island Historical Society, which he supported financially.

Davis was a small, quiet man with a large nose. He reminded some people of the eponymous Mr. Chips in James Hilton's novel, while others called him "Dr. Bug," though he had only a high school education and was, entomologically speaking, largely self-taught. A keen observer, patient and attentive to detail, he loved nothing more than being outdoors, so much so that when he was a young man, his mother reported, with some distress, that he preferred bug watching to girl watching. He married in 1900, but his wife died a year later and thereafter he remained single, living out the rest of his days no more than 200 feet from where he was born. His working life was tame: twenty-six uninspiring years at the New York Produce Exchange, and he retired at age forty-three to pursue his scientific interests full time. Although temperamentally mild and gentle, Davis was no fool financially and managed to amass a decent fortune, which—no surprise—he bequeathed to civic and scientific causes.

His passion was cicadas, commonly (and inaccurately) called seventeen-year locusts, which engaged his intellect, his imagination, and his sympathies. These insects were not the Biblical variety sent to plague Egypt nor the devouring hordes from whom seagulls delivered the Mormons in Utah; his insects of choice were the harmless though noisy cicadas of the genera *Tibicen* and *Magicicada*. Davis measured out his life in the latter's cyclical reappearance. Born two years after the emergence of Brood 2 in 1860, he witnessed them first when he was fifteen years old. (Periodical cicadas are grouped into Broods according to the year they emerge from the earth. The group most common to Staten Island has been designated Brood 2.)

Davis saw his cicadas again in 1894, 1911, and 1928. Each time, their emergence energized him to produce scientific papers on their habits, appearance, and taxonomic classification. People sent him specimens to identify; *Tibicen davisi* has been named for him. Davis admired the process by which they emerged soft and moist from their shells and climbed up tree trunks to dry. He also admired what he saw as the quiet, contemplative life they led for seventeen years in the darkness of the earth, safe from the anxieties of the world above. Cicadas inspired him to the end. About six months before his death, he wrote to a friend that growing old was no fun, and that some people turned to drink or the Bible in confronting their losses, but others instead studied cicadas.

He died on 22 January 1945, just a few months before the cicadas of Brood 2 again emerged on Staten Island.

THE WILLIAM T. DAVIS WILDLIFE REFUGE

The Refuge (*map p. 260, C3*), abutting Freshkills Park, is one of the oldest stretches of protected land in the Greenbelt. Davis long hoped to bring a park to Staten Island, and for him the best park was a patch of woods left as nature had planned it, though maybe with a few paths. And this is, more or less, what the William T. Davis Wildlife Refuge turned out to be. Sixth largest of New York City's more than 1,700 parks, it harbors herons, egrets, cormorants, snapping turtles, and muskrats. Its marshes and ponds filter water and provide natural flood control. The Greenbelt Native Plant Center, a thirteen–acre greenhouse, nursery, and seed bank located on the former Mohlenhoff family farm (1911–92), provides native plants and seeds propagated from local plant populations to be used in restoring natural areas.

Henry David Thoreau on Staten Island

Henry David Thoreau (1817–62) arrived on Staten Island in May 1843, in search of a vocation. His mentor, Ralph Waldo Emerson, had finagled him a job tutoring his nephews, but Thoreau also wanted to be close to New York to further his writing career. Though he could be prickly and standoffish, the young Thoreau thought the job a good fit, an acquiescence unusual for him. Waldo Emerson sent his brother William a note warning that Thoreau had a bold and original mind, but some possibly annoying eccentricities as well.

Thoreau found the Island beautiful. He took long walks ("tramps," William T. Davis would have called them), sometimes collecting Indian arrowheads, but always admiring the trees and flowers. He climbed Grymes Hill and enjoyed the panoramic view; he noticed wild garlic growing in the fields. At the end of May, he wrote to his sister, describing the Island's fertility, as had the early explorers centuries before: the air was fragrant with cedar; the trees were large and beautiful; cherry trees bloomed in every dooryard; in fact, the whole island was like a garden.

About a month after his arrival, he witnessed seventeen-year cicadas emerging from the ground and commented on their din, so noisy that passing ships could hear them. Unlike Davis, who would find them harmless, even reassuring, Thoreau believed that the cicadas damaged the trees, burrowing under the bark to deposit their eggs. It was the same brood whose second return thirty-four years later would enthrall the teenage William T. Davis (*see above*).

Above all Thoreau loved the sea. He spent hours with his spy glass focused on ships heading up the Narrows, taking on their pilots, proceeding toward the Quarantine. He walked the beach, impressed by the sweep of the view, taking in everything he saw: water and seaweed, shad nets drying on the sand; fishing boats out in the surf or dragged up onto the sand by oxen. Not even the smell of the dead fish, horses, and hogs washed up on the beach offended him. Half-wild dogs haunted the shore, perhaps drawn by the carrion. Sometimes Thoreau in his lonely wanderings would come across the carcass of a horse or ox washed up on the sand and see a dog slinking away, its mouth full of the animal's entrails. Writing about Cape Cod years later, he recalled a time on Staten Island when he had rescued a small dog attacked by a pack of larger ones. He stoned the pack, possibly inviting the dogs to turn on him. But when he walked on the same beach the next day, the dog he had saved was quick to snarl at him. The recollection set him musing on ingratitude.

Despite the beauty of his surroundings, Thoreau's sojourn on Staten Island was unhappy. He didn't much care for seven-year-old Willie Emerson, whom he nevertheless took on long hikes in the woods and fields. He was sometimes ill and often homesick, but the deepest source of his discontent was his employer. William Emerson was a lawyer, a successful judge, a respected citizen, but according to Thoreau void of intellectual or spiritual life, a business man, nothing more, head of a family whose arid life revolved around visitors' cards and social events. The only thing in the household with any vitality, thought Thoreau, were the shells on the mantelpiece.

In later years Thoreau would become a social thinker and a political activist as well as an environmentalist and a close observer of nature. He left Staten Island in December 1843 and did not return.

Frederick Law Olmsted on Staten Island

Frederick Law Olmsted (1822–1903), landscape architect, ecologist, journalist, urban planner, and all-around humanitarian, has reserved himself a place in the hearts of New Yorkers for his designs of Central Park in Manhattan and Prospect Park in Brooklyn. He got there, professionally speaking, by way of Staten Island. As a young man, Olmsted lived on Staten Island—only for a few years, but while he was there his career began to find direction. Only the farmhouse where he lived and a few stands of trees remain from his sojourn.

A late bloomer blessed with an indulgent and well-heeled father, Olmsted arrived in Staten Island in 1848 when he was twenty-six, fired up over the prospect of using the latest technological and horticultural discoveries to become a "scientific" farmer. He had already tried his hand at surveying (as the pupil of a topographical engineer), had clerked with a Manhattan silk importer (briefly and miserably), sailed to China and back as a common sailor aboard a merchant vessel (also miserably but not briefly: the voyage lasted a full year), and enrolled at Yale (briefly again; chemistry, but little else, fascinated him).

Olmsted described his boyhood self as active, inventive, impulsive, and enterprising, and these traits followed him perhaps in attenuated form, into adulthood. His formal education was slipshod and haphazard. His mother died when he was four and his father farmed him out to a succession of Congregational ministers in nearby Connecticut towns—some kind, some cruel but most of them indifferent to Frederick's education. On the other hand, young Frederick had plenty of free time to ramble around the woods. He came to love the outdoors, and his deep appreciation for the New England landscape became a guiding principle of his life. As an adult he attempted to transfer the values he found in the natural world to the cities he saw growing up around him. Incidentally, he became an omnivorous reader and an admirer of science. (But he never learned to spell properly, and he never was much good at making money.)

When he was in his twenties, farming seized his imagination. Before he actually took up the profession he declared in a letter, with typical Olmstedian enthusiasm though without much concrete evidence, that farming was of all professions the most satisfying, the most conducive to happiness; put simply, farmers were the happiest of men. For him, agriculture had also a spiritual dimension.

Yes, the farmer enjoyed the material benefits of his labor and profited his fellow man, but because he cultivated the natural world, God's handiwork, he also cultivated his own aesthetic sense and his moral capacity.

Before he landed on Staten Island, Olmsted had spent a bitter year working a windswept, rocky plot in Guilford, Connecticut, but the harsh conditions and his standoffish Yankee neighbors defeated him. His ever-generous father then bought him better fields to till, 130 acres on a gentle slope facing Raritan Bay on the southern part of the Island. The property had originally belonged to a Dutch farmer named Petrus Tesschenmaker (spelled various ways), who had constructed a one-room stone house in 1685. Subsequent owners had expanded it, plastering the walls, adding a second story, bedrooms, and a porch. Most recently it had belonged to Dr. Samuel Akerly, a physician, gentleman farmer, scientist, and philanthropist.

An advertisement in the *New York Daily Tribune* described the property in glowing terms: situated on Raritan Bay, the house offered a view of unsurpassed beauty—the Lower Bay and all the passing ships. Fruit trees and grape vines graced the property, which had a pond, barns, and a large, new house. The ad was accurate about the view, but less so about the condition of the property. The grounds were shabby; the pond was little more than a mud hole. The barns stood uncomfortably close to the house. The whole place was dirty and disorderly enough to please the most avid seeker of rural simplicity.

As soon as Olmsted arrived, he started tinkering. He renamed the place Tosomock Farm, presumably a corruption of Tesschenmaker (it is now the Olmsted-Beil House; *see p. 211*). He replanted the wheat fields with cabbages, turnips, lima beans, grapes, and peaches. He imported specimen trees from France, planting walnuts, ginkgoes, and Cedars of Lebanon, some of which remain. He began cautious forays into what would become "landscape architecture," moving outbuildings away from the house to improve the view, re-routing the driveway, transforming the mud hole into a pleasant pond. He also sharpened his administrative skills, hiring farmhands and establishing exacting schedules for the work, requiring, for example, that tools be replaced in their appointed spots at the end of each day before the workers could go home to dinner. His efforts at overseeing perhaps forty farmhands anticipated the days he would later spend as Central Park's chief administrator supervising as many as 20,000 workers.

Olmsted became a founder of the Staten Island Agricultural Society in 1849 and also served as corresponding secretary, an early instance of his social activism. The position bore fruit professionally since William H. Vanderbilt also belonged to the society. Decades later, Vanderbilt would hire Olmsted to design the grounds of the Vanderbilt family mausoleum (*see p. 144*). And his son, George Washington Vanderbilt II, would hire Olmsted to lay out the grounds of "Biltmore," his vast North Carolina estate.

The years at Tosomock Farm constituted a halcyon period in Olmsted's young life. But true to form, he soon became restless and bored. When he left Staten Island in 1850 to tour cities, parks, and estates of England, he had already begun to develop the talents and skills that would serve him and the American landscape for the rest of his life. Olmsted returned to Staten Island two decades later. In his absence—the years that encompassed the Civil War, its aftermath, large-scale industrialization and migration to cities—Olmsted would repeat the restless pattern of his youth, moving from job to job. He undertook each task enthusiastically, sometimes worked himself to exhaustion, became bored or disillusioned, and moved on to the next enthusiasm. Nevertheless, he remained passionately committed to his vision of social justice, his belief that in the struggle to achieve it, Nature was a guiding and civilizing force.

In 1870, by then a man of substance and reputation, Olmsted was asked to join a New York State commission to submit plans to make Staten Island more attractive as a suburban community. At the time he was living in Clifton, commuting by ferry to Brooklyn, where Prospect Park was emerging from the unkempt fields of Flatbush. Despite Staten Island's reputation for malaria, Olmsted believed that it could be made desirable. He and his co-authors (and it seems that Olmsted did most of the work) offered a fourteen-point scheme for upgrading ferries, roads, and parks, and for controlling flooding and improving drainage of low places, which he thought might alleviate malaria (though the parasitic basis for the disease was not yet recognized). The document was far ahead of its time, touching systematically on several environmental concerns. But Staten Island's villages couldn't act in concert, especially given the estimated cost of $2–4 million, so improvements were made piecemeal if at all. The plan was forgotten for almost a century, when it was discovered that Olmsted had recommended the creation of a chain of parks, an idea that eventually blossomed into the notion of Staten Island's Greenbelt.

Today Olmsted is remembered as the father of landscape architecture, a tireless advocate for open spaces and parks for rich and poor alike, the designer of landscapes for the rich and famous, an urban planner, and a writer—a visionary man and a tireless worker. In the long run, his years on Staten Island had more impact on him and his personal future than, alas, he did on the Island and its urban future. Malaria no longer plagues Islanders (though mosquitoes do), traffic snarls still cause widespread irritation, and flooding of low areas causes real grief. He would, however, be pleased about the parks.

THE STATEN ISLAND GREENBELT

Staten Island's Greenbelt is remarkable within New York City: 2,800 contiguous acres of woodlands, ponds, hills, meadows, and swamps, running mid-Island from the Staten Island Expressway south to Arthur Kill Road and then curving north again to encompass the 2,000 acres of Freshkills Park now under construction. Over the last three and a half decades, the Greenbelt has pieced together a boy scout camp, a country club, a swamp, a cemetery, former hospital grounds, and city parks. Its existence is another example—maybe the prime example on Staten Island—of a David-and-Goliath struggle won through the determination and political savvy of local advocates fighting against apparently invincible enemies.

The Battle for Camp High Rock

High Rock Park (*map p. 261, D3*) is the Greenbelt's centerpiece, its spiritual if not geographical core, though not its first officially preserved patch of land (that honor belongs to the William T. Davis Wildlife Refuge of 1928). As New York parks go, High Rock is young, dedicated in 1965, almost a century after Manhattan's Central Park. But its creation did not come without a struggle.

In 1951, the New York Council of Girl Scouts purchased ninety-four acres in what is now the Greenbelt. Up until then, humanity had trodden lightly here, for the steep ravines and swampy hollows made the land unsuitable for development. Although the occupying British and Hessian troops during the Revolution had chopped down the forests for firewood, second-growth forest arose, and in the nineteenth century a few loggers and hardscrabble farmers lived there. But for eons High Rock remained more or less as nature had arranged it.

Then, in 1930, the Boy Scouts assembled 143 acres for a camp. They bought a former chicken farm, some Vanderbilt land, and 100 acres from the estate of the architect Ernest Flagg. The camp thrived. Wealthy benefactors contributed: Nathan Orbach, the department store magnate; Thomas Watson Jr., second president of IBM and eleventh national president of the Boy Scouts of America; and industrialist William T. Pouch, for whom the camp is named. As many as 75,000 Boy Scouts arrived yearly to sleep in lean-tos, tie knots, build fires, and learn the do's and don'ts of good citizenship. In 1951, aware that a six-lane highway was on the drawing board and that its route would take it right through the heart of Pouch Camp, the Boy Scout Council of Greater New York sold off sixty-two acres on the less desirable side of the road to the Girl Scouts. The price was $35,000, about $600 an acre.

By 1959, construction for the Verrazano-Narrows Bridge was underway, opening the prospect of development. Mrs. Howard Phipps, president of the Girl Scout Council of Greater New York and a woman of wealth and social standing (Mr. Howard Phipps was a former president of US Steel), knew opportunity when she saw it. The land beneath the Girl Scout camp was now worth $18,000 an acre, representing a 3,000 percent gain in eight years. Rumors (possibly planted, to make selling appear the better choice) began to buzz about with the virulence of Staten Island's infamous mosquitoes: bullet holes pocked one of the buildings, peeping toms had been spotted stalking through the woods. Clearly it was time to get out. In 1964, the Girl Scout Council entered into an agreement to sell Camp High Rock to New Dorp Gardens, Inc. for $1,067,000. ("Gardens" in this context meant "garden apartments," not flower beds.) New Dorp Gardens, Inc. quickly began digging foundations and pouring concrete.

That should have been the end of High Rock as open space, but it wasn't. Neither the Girl Scouts, nor the Boy Scouts, nor some years later, Robert Moses, counted on Gretta Moulton, who had followed her husband to Staten Island from Massachusetts, where she had been a mover and shaker in the Girl Scouts. She simply picked up where she had left off. Her job, as she first saw it, was to save Camp High Rock as open space and she and other environmental activists responded to New Dorp Gardens, Inc. by applying for a change in zoning to prohibit garden apartments. While they knew that this was merely stalling for time—the developers could simply put up single family houses instead—the ploy worked.

Meanwhile, attitudes toward conservation were changing. Stewart Udall, secretary of the interior under President John F. Kennedy, warned of impending disaster in *The Quiet Crisis* (1963), his watershed book on environmentalism in the US. Gretta Moulton, who had originally set out simply to save High Rock Camp, soon saw its acreage as a vital part of a projected park that could stretch much of the length of Staten Island, linking lands still free from development.

The Greenbelters mobilized City and State agencies to raise more than $1,300,000 to compensate New Dorp Gardens, Inc. In July 1965, High Rock Conservation Center was dedicated as an official NYC park.

So it seemed that High Rock was saved, but the notion of a highway—Richmond Parkway—still lurked in Robert Moses' mind. In fact, in that same year, 1965, the New York State Department of Public Works awarded the first construction contract. Thus it was, at the dedication of the High Rock Nature Center, as everyone was busy cutting ceremonial ribbons and basking in success, that Robert Hagenhofer, chairman of the Staten Island Citizens Planning Committee and a man with an oratorical flair, stood up and pointed to a map showing the proposed expressway hard by the edge of the park. This park, he said, is going to be one-quarter highway. Jaws dropped.

The battle against Richmond Parkway

The struggle began again. The Greenbelt activists released a position paper urging that Richmond Parkway be re-routed further west. Moses refused. He called the conservationists "daisy pickers," a scathing precursor of "tree huggers." The highway would make the area more accessible to police protection, he said, without which the Greenbelt could become an urban jungle where people's safety at night wouldn't be worth a plugged nickel.

Normally a consummate strategist, Moses would have done well to say nothing and to let the activists' position paper gather dust in the obscurity of some file drawer. Instead, his public remarks drew attention to the possible destruction of the Greenbelt. By 1967, Moses had bullied too many for too long and was losing favor with the press and with officials who had long supported him. Time was now on the side of the conservationists.

Ironically, Frederick Law Olmsted became the savior of the Greenbelt. In his "Report to the Staten Island Improvement Commission of a Preliminary Scheme of Improvements," Olmsted had pointed to two key drawbacks of the Island: its poor roads and its nasty reputation as a breeding ground for malaria. In proposing locations for new roads, Olmsted described the Island's steep central ridge, the "back bone of the island," impractical for horse-drawn vehicles or building lots. In another section of the report, Olmsted proposed draining marshy spots with an elaborate network of underground pipes graded so that ground water would flow to outfalls near the shore. In connection with this plan, he suggested a reservoir system and a park, maybe four miles long, near the center of the Island.

A century later, one of the Greenbelt conservationists, Bradford Green, came across the Olmsted recommendations and stitched them together making it look as if the father of American landscape architecture was actually proposing the Greenbelt. The activists invited celebrities and politicians to hike on the "Olmsted Trailway," keeping the controversy in the public eye. Meanwhile, competing city agencies hemmed and hawed, proposing different routes for the highway, while Moses himself remained adamant, refusing to move his planned highway an inch in any direction. Moses' enemies continued to chip away at his power, and in 1966 stripped him of his position as arterial coordinator of the City.

The end of the road

Construction began in 1965 on the southern section of Richmond Parkway, the part that didn't impinge on the Greenbelt, but halted in 1972. The next year a statewide $3.5-billion transportation bill was defeated, stopping Richmond Parkway short. Today, that southern portion of it (renamed Korean Veterans Highway) ends at Richmond Avenue. At its proposed beginning, between exits 12 and 13 of the Staten Island Expressway, empty ramps swerve off into the woods and until 2012, an overpass to nowhere hovered above the highway. The Greenbelt, for now, remains intact. Within it stands a monument to Robert Moses' failed effort at road building, a 200-foot pile of excavated rock and earth from whose summit you can enjoy a panoramic view of the Greenbelt and beyond. It is named Moses' Mountain (*map p. 261, D3*).

FRESH KILLS: FROM MARSH TO DUMP

Before 1948, when it became a dumping ground for New York's garbage, Fresh Kills (*map p. 260, B4*) was mostly salt marsh inundated by the tides flowing through the Arthur Kill. Through it snaked a system of tidal creeks that drained the Island's central hills and emptied into the Arthur Kill. It also embraced upland, some of it actively farmed, some of it abandoned and reverting to its natural vegetation. For centuries Fresh Kills had remained more or less the same. Native Americans had hunted, fished, and gathered shell-fish here, leaving behind tools and campsites with mid-dens of oyster and clam shells. The Dutch who arrived in the seventeenth century cut salt hay in the marshes, using it for mulch (no weed seeds) and bedding for livestock. Cargo ships traversed Fresh Kills Creek and Richmond Creek, but the waterways remained clean enough for fish-ing until the twentieth century.

In the nineteenth century, Martin Johnson Heade and other landscapists associated with the Hudson River School found the salt marshes beautiful enough to paint, but by the early years of the twentieth, tidal wetlands in the popular mind had fallen to the status of noxious, mos-quito-infested wastelands; at low tide the mud flats looked unsightly and smelled like rotten eggs. The wet soil pre-cluded building much of anything on them. And so they became targets for landfill.

Landfill operations in New York dated back to Dutch days on Manhattan Island, when the shoreline was pushed out into the East River; New Yorkers centuries later had used landfill to create the land on which the World Trade Center stands. Robert Moses prided himself on having cleaned up a notorious ash dump in Queens and on using the land thereby created for the grounds of the 1939 World's Fair and for parkland thereafter. It was Moses who would become the moving force behind the Fresh Kills Landfill.

In the 1930s, as part of his master plan for arterial roadways around New York City, Moses saw the uninhabited Fresh Kills marsh as instrumental in his scheme to link a (future) bridge across the Narrows with the Goethals Bridge, the Bayonne Bridge, and the Outerbridge Crossing. If he could fill the marsh, he could create a base for the road, reduce the cost of bridges crossing the creeks, and tap funds from a priority City budget reserved for urgent civic needs. He secretly suggested to the head of NYC Sanitation that disposal operations move to Fresh Kills.

Ten years passed, during which Moses successfully implemented other bridge and roadway projects. In 1943, again secretly, Moses convinced the borough president to have plans drawn up for filling the Fresh Kills meadows and submitted the plans to Mayor Fiorello La Guardia, with a request for adoption. The plans remained under wraps until July 1945.

When the plan became public, irate Staten Islanders descended on City Hall. Call it what you will, they protested; the proposed landfill is nothing but a garbage dump. They told of sickening odors at the earlier Great Kills landfill and of children chased by dump rats gone astray. In response, the mayor agreed to tour the dump at Great Kills and, unsurprisingly, found that it stank, even after being sprayed with a deodorant of castor oil and benzene. The touring dignitaries refused the invitation of the locals to spend the night on the dump site.

But this was the 1940s. The protesters didn't stand a chance; Moses had his way. The first garbage arrived in 1948.

Though Moses promised that "raw" garbage would be taken to Fresh Kills only for three years while incinerators were built elsewhere, he soon asked for four more years. He painted a rosy picture of the dump: the garbage was too tightly compressed to harbor rats; the larvicide would kill insects before they were hatched; the earth cover would smother the odor. The reality, however, was rancid, not rosy. Fresh Kills continued to accept garbage until 1996 and it smelled terrible. It had rats and bugs. The garbage mounds rose to contain an estimated 150 million tons of solid waste.

By the mid-1990s, Fresh Kills was the only landfill still operating in New York City. The mounds of garbage grew taller than the Statue of Liberty, more massive than the Pyramids of Giza and the Great Wall of China, eventually becoming the largest man-made object on the face of the earth. During peak periods (1986–87), 29,000 tons of "fresh" garbage arrived every day. Tug boats nosed garbage scows into the Arthur Kill. Long-necked cranes with steel-toothed clamshell buckets clawed up huge globs of garbage and spat them into open carts, which were dragged uphill by tractors. Giant steel-treaded bulldozers pushed garbage here and there, crawling up garbage mountains, descending through garbage valleys. Overhead circled hundreds of black-backed gulls, swooping and diving for their next meal. For miles the air smelled of rotting household refuse, industrial and hospital waste, and whatever else the City had jettisoned. Staten Islanders in neighboring communities complained bitterly; after all, they were living with forty percent of the entire city's garbage, not just their own.

The local and state governments finally caved in to civic and environmental protests. In 1996, the governor, the mayor, and the borough president issued an order to close the landfill on 31 December 2001, but after the attack on the World Trade Center on September 11, the order was amended to allow Fresh Kills to receive the debris from the fallen towers. About 1.2 million tons of material were deposited on a forty-eight-acre site and for ten months workers screened it, looking for human remains and objects that might identify the victims. The remains were brought to the medical examiner's for identification and the rest of the material was placed in a fifty-acre area on the West Mound and buried beneath clean soil.

Freshkills Park: rising from the Dump

If Frederick Law Olmsted's Central Park expressed the enlightened social and cultural ideals of the mid-nineteenth century, then James Corner's Field Operations' plans for

Freshkills Park do something similar for the twenty-first. Best known for the design of the High Line on an unused rail spur in Manhattan, Corner, who was chosen in an international competition, sees the park not only as traditional green space but as symbolic of twenty-first-century notions of using technology to heal the earth.

Olmsted's sculpted landscape in Central Park, with its ninety-five miles of subterranean drainage pipe, man-made hills, and imported trees, was intended to improve what nature had wrought—a rocky, muddy patch beset with squatters' huts, pigs, and swill. To make the new landscape, 10,500 men moved 1,444,800 cubic yards of earth, and excavated 198,000 cubic yards of rock using 132.5 tons of gunpowder. In addition, they planted 150,000 trees. Freshkills Park, on the site of the Fresh Kills Sanitary Landfill, reclaims a naturally beautiful area degraded by a dispiriting combination of human ambition, waste, and fecklessness. (But where does the garbage go now? *See overleaf.*)

Ironically, Freshkills is only about half a mile as the crow flies from Olmsted's Staten Island farm. He could have walked there. And perhaps he did, but he could not have envisioned what is happening now or the challenges facing the present designers. When the park is finished, thirty or so years hence, Freshkills (the name of the park is one word; the name of the previous dump and the early salt meadows is two) will offer just about everything you could wish for in a park. You will be able to walk, run, paddle, pedal, ride horseback, and ski cross-country somewhere in its 2,200 acres. You will find places to toss Frisbees; hit, kick, or dribble balls; observe birds; contemplate nature; enjoy art; and watch grass grow (or at least watch the landscape rejuvenate itself from special viewing berms).

GARBAGE DISPOSAL AFTER 2001

The ten thousand tons of household trash generated daily by New York City did not disappear when the Fresh Kills Landfill closed. In 2001, the City began trucking most of its garbage to other, more distant, landfills at an estimated cost of $95 a ton. The attendant traffic congestion, noise, and air pollution led to a plan in 2006 to transport most of the trash by train and barge, and to have each borough handle its own waste, with a more equitable distribution of transfer stations, most of which are currently in poorer neighborhoods. At present the City is seeking to facilitate state-of-the-art, high tech facilities that will convert trash to energy by means of anaerobic digestion, gasification or hydrolysis, rather than incineration. And since only fifteen percent of New York's trash gets recycled compared with as much as forty percent in some European cities, programs to reduce waste and increase recycling also offer some hope of dealing with this gargantuan problem.

Only forty-five percent of Freshkills Park rests on landfill; the remainder is salt marsh and tidal flats, freshwater wetlands, creeks, meadows, swamp forest, and woodland. Nevertheless, the four former garbage mounds dominate the landscape and will become the centerpieces of separate park areas. The mounds, right now at least, are not quite like anything seen elsewhere—brooding and brown in the winter months, increasingly green with each returning spring.

The two largest mounds have been capped and are becoming West Park and East Park. The other two mounds, which form the central spine of the site, the South Mound and the North Mound, have been closed since the mid-1990s. In the center of Freshkills a fifth park, the Confluence, will be designed around the area where Main Creek and Richmond Creek join briefly before dividing again around Isle of Meadows.

Each of the five park areas will have its own presence, depending on its topography and location. The **North Park**, for example, abutting the William T. Davis Wildlife Refuge, will remain largely natural, extending acreage of the refuge; it will have trails and platforms for bird watching. In the **West Park**, where the material from the fallen World Trade Center is buried, a monumental earthwork on the hilltop will commemorate the attack and provide a place for contemplation. The work as planned will take the shape of two earth forms lying side by side on a slight incline, each the length (height) and width of the Twin

Towers. From the top of the rise, you will be able to look east to Manhattan across a wildflower meadow to the spot where the towers stood. The **Confluence** will offer a visitor center, canoe and kayak rentals, a fishing pier, a restaurant, and other amenities. Garbage scows converted to floating gardens and old dump machinery installed as "found" art will remind you of pre-park Fresh Kills. **East Park** will have meadows, lawns and trails, recreation fields and perhaps a large-scale art installation, boardwalks over wetlands, and educational exhibits. Maybe even, in ten or twenty years, a golf course. **South Park**, with acres of flat, dry lowlands, is slated for soccer and tennis fields, an equestrian facility with stables and bridle paths, and trails for mountain biking. You will be able to climb the mound and check out the view. Around the park's perimeter, state-of-the-art playgrounds will serve adjacent Staten Island neighborhoods, the first of which, Schmul Park, named for the family who donated their farmland for the playground in 1939, opened in 2012.

The greening of the Dump

Just as the Fresh Kills Landfill was a colossal disaster, Freshkills Park will be a monumental act of ecological contrition. Everything possible will be done to ensure that Freshkills is as "green" as possible, both literally and metaphorically. Buildings will take advantage of passive heating and cooling systems; some will have "green" roofs or photovoltaic light systems; some will be recycled from facilities once used by the NYC Department of Sanitation.

The garbage has been covered, but the plants currently thriving in the thin, weak soil, are tall reedy phragmites and ailanthus trees (the legendary kind that grew in Brooklyn), and mugwort—invasive species that survive in wretched environments. The soil will be enriched and when the infrastructure is completed, the mounds will be replanted with native grasses and flowers grown from locally collected seed treated to ensure its hardiness. Local species of trees grown in pots and nurtured to maturity will be transplanted throughout the park.

Energy from methane is already being captured and sold for home heating. In 2012, the city solicited bids for constructing a wind and solar farm on a 75-acre plot.

All this will take time, an estimated thirty years. The first park projects opened in 2012, but the capping of the fourth mound—a process that takes six or seven years—is still in progress. It will also cost a lot of money. Already various city and state agencies have allotted some $120 million for continuing the closure of the landfill, and an additional $150 million for maintenance thereafter. Right now it is assumed that the annual cost to maintain Freshkills Park when completed will be between $15,000 and $30,000 per acre (multiplied times 2,200), even though eighty percent of the site will be meadow, woodland, wetland, and water. It has not been easy, and it will not be cheap. But after half a century of stench and filth, Staten Islanders are more than ready for the greening of the Dump.

WOMEN OF STATEN ISLAND

Alice Austen—Jacques Marchais and the Museum of Tibetan Art—Staten Island Saints

Neither Alice Austen (1866–1952) nor Jacques Marchais (1887–1948) is well-known in the larger world, though both were remarkable characters. Their lives followed opposite trajectories: Alice Austen coasted through life until old age; Jacques Marchais scrabbled her way up from poverty to realize her most cherished ambition but did not live long thereafter to enjoy it.

ALICE AUSTEN

Alice Austen, a pioneering woman photographer whose work documents Staten Island during gentler, more leisured times, lived a life that went from riches to rags. Born to comfort, she enjoyed the privileges of money and position until financial catastrophe overwhelmed her old age. Perhaps handicapped by the habits of wealth but still resisting every step of the way, she slid into poverty. Only at the very last came an improbable uptick in her fortunes; her life ended like that of the opera heroine, who, frail and pallid, gets to sing one last glorious aria before the curtain falls. There was, however, nothing pallid about Alice Austen.

Elizabeth Alice Austen was born in less than happy circumstances. Her father, Edward Stopford Munn, abandoned his wife when she was pregnant and hurried back to his native England. When little Alice was baptized, she was given her mother's maiden name; later on friends could provoke her by calling her Alice Munn.

Alice and her mother moved into the Austen family home, "Clear Comfort," originally a Dutch farmhouse built in about 1690 (*map p. 261, F2*). Austen's grandfather had bought the house in 1844 and remodeled it as a Victorian Gothic cottage. Here Alice lived, the adored only child in a household with five adults—her mother, her grandparents, and an aunt and uncle. When she was ten, the uncle, a sea captain, loaned her a camera and gave her a couple of lessons on how to use it. Another uncle, a chemistry professor, seems to have taught her about developing and printing; her parents built her a darkroom in an upstairs closet. The rest she figured out by herself.

Many of her early photos are the kind expected of women of her time and class; they show Alice and her companions—young men and women—playing sports, dressed for social events, or simply acting "larky"—pretending to be drunk on tea or playing pranks in a cemetery. She photographed her home: its rooms cluttered with *objets d'art*, antique furniture, and knickknacks; its expansive garden with an exuberant wisteria clinging to the roof; the Victorian "gingerbread" decorating the eaves. She photographed herself in stiff, bustled dresses or outfitted in a Spanish costume for a dance recital.

Some of her work, however, is less conventional. While female photographers in her day were expected to limit themselves to domestic subjects and to romanticize even those, Alice Austen looked beyond her own walls. Her photos are unsentimental, documentary. They are not intended to persuade, as were those of the social reformers Jacob Riis or Lewis Hine; they simply show what was there. Had she been born later, or perhaps had she found it necessary to earn her living earlier in her life, she might have been a photojournalist. She depicted workers and street people: newsboys, immigrants, street sweepers, shoeshine men, and Italian organ grinders in New York; black oyster shuckers in Maryland. She recorded newsworthy events—the flotilla welcoming Admiral George Dewey home from the Spanish American War, the funeral cortege of Ulysses S. Grant, celebration of the end of World War I—and was fascinated by the Quarantine (on Hoffman and Swinburne Islands at the time), where she repeatedly hauled her heavy camera and its accessories to photograph the disinfecting chambers, laboratory apparatus, even the toilets.

Her life, like her photos, was both ordinary and unconventional. As a young woman, Austen was athletic and bold, a strong swimmer, and a skillful sailor. She was gifted with curiosity and a talent for things mechanical. She drove her green Franklin car over rutted, unpaved roads as far as Ohio, changing tires herself and sometimes making simple repairs. During World War I she joined the Motor Corps, transporting injured soldiers from the docks to local hospitals. On the other hand, her private school education segued into a life of parties and genteel sporting events with Cunards, Vanderbilts, and other gilded Staten Island families. As a privileged woman, she gardened, volunteered for the Historical Society, and traveled here and abroad.

At a time when doctors proscribed exercise as dangerous for women, she dove right in, so to speak. Her single paid commission was a series of photos illustrating a how-to book on bicycling for women, a sport of dubious propriety (you couldn't ride a bike side saddle) and suspect healthfulness. The author of *Bicycling for Ladies*, her friend Violet Ward, noted the sport's subversive undertones: cycling, said Violet to her readers, offers the pleasure of going where you want to go, because you want to go there. It reveals women's "powers" and offers them a greater freedom of movement. Needless to say, Alice loved cycling.

Alice Austen and Gertrude Tate

Alice Austen, who never married, had a fifty-year domestic relationship with Gertrude Tate, something then called a "Boston marriage." Late in her life she explained that she had remained single because she was "too good to get married," by which she meant too athletic, too handy, and too independent to appeal to men. Nor did her father's desertion and her mother's bitterness en-

hance her view of men as lifetime partners. The friendship with Gertrude Tate began in 1899 in the Catskills,
where Gertrude, then living in Brooklyn and supporting
her mother and sister by teaching kindergarten, was re-
cuperating from typhoid fever. Alice was visiting friends.
Gertrude's family disapproved, calling her attachment to
Alice "wrong devotion," and Gertrude did not move into
"Clear Comfort" for another eighteen years.

No one can know for certain whether the relationship
was sexual. Some of Austen's photos do explore gender
roles, for example showing her and her girl friends in
bed together or dressed as men striking nonchalant male
poses, but Victorian female friendship permitted a degree
of intimacy that would not be accepted as heterosexual
behavior today. Nevertheless, Austen's photos are sug-
gestive and the gay community has interpreted them as
overtly sexual.

The fall from grace

For many years Austen's life continued swimmingly,
though her finances grew leaner after her grandfather died
in 1894. Still, she could afford to attend the Metropolitan
Opera, to lunch at the Colony Club in Manhattan, and
to participate in events appropriate for someone listed in
the New York Social Register. The financial picture dark-
ened after World War I: the inheritance dwindled but the
cost of the opera tickets and the club memberships did
not. The neighborhood around "Clear Comfort" changed.

The waterfront, once the playground of yachtsmen, became industrial. Local children, no longer the offspring of the socially privileged, chucked rocks at the porcelain urns Austen had artfully placed about the yard. Married friends moved away and single ones grew unsociable. She and Gertrude felt increasingly isolated. Unable to live on the income from her diminished capital, Austen turned to a stock broker she knew and allowed him to invest her capital—on margin in dicey and now long-forgotten enterprises. In 1929, the investments plummeted. Believing the crash only temporary, she made a second disastrous decision—to mortgage the house—financing one last European vacation for herself and Gertrude.

And yet her one asset, "Clear Comfort," remained valuable, not because of its historic elegance but ironically because of its proximity to the docks. Austen got offers to sell, ranging from $100,000 in 1918, to $175,000 a few years later; she turned them all down. Flat.

Gertrude tried to pull them through by giving ballroom dancing lessons at acceptable venues and "charm" courses over the radio. Austen begged distant relatives for money and rented out the upstairs apartment. Piecemeal she sold off the family antiques and silver, usually at bargain basement prices. The bank foreclosed in 1934, but let the women remain for a minuscule rent. Ten years later, Bankers Trust sold the house for $7,500, a measly sum even considering that its value had plummeted when the neighborhood was re-zoned as residential. The buyer was a Miss Grace Mandia, whose family owned a tavern on Bay Street.

In 1945, Alice and Gertrude were evicted.

Unwilling to see her possessions auctioned publicly, Austen asked a New Jersey furniture dealer to appraise the contents of the house, for which he offered $600, a "disgusting bargain" according a friend, who would have brokered a better deal had she asked. As the dealer was carrying off Austen's possessions, Loring McMillen from the Staten Island Historical Society appeared on the scene to find the household in disarray and Austen in hysterics. She had verbally agreed with the dealer to pile the things she wanted in one room and to allow him to take the rest, but when he appeared with his truck, she ran about the rooms stuffing objects into her apron pocket and carrying them into the "preservation" room. McMillen summoned the Historical Society's lawyer.

Upstairs, McMillen found a dust-covered pile of cardboard boxes, holding stacks of 4 x 5-inch glass plates, each in a brown paper envelope. Holding them up to the light, he saw old street scenes, horses and buggies, Victorian houses. With Austen's permission, he took the negatives to the Historical Society, where they were stored in the basement to gather more dust. These 3,000 or so plates appear to represent about half the total in the house; the other half ended up with the dealer and have been lost.

Years passed. Alice and Gertrude moved to a small apartment on Bay Street, where Gertrude adjusted to the new circumstances and Alice grew increasingly miserable, her arthritis progressing until she could no longer walk. Gertrude fell, broke her wrist, and had to move in with her family in Queens. Alice, unable to live independently, was moved to a series of nursing homes where her cantankerous behavior earned her no friends. In 1950, destitute, she signed over her remaining possessions to Gertrude and declared herself legally a pauper so that she could become a ward of the city. Her next stop was the New York Farm Colony, the poorhouse (*see p. 194*). She had hit rock bottom.

Meanwhile, in 1948, C. Coapes Brinley, a volunteer at the Staten Island Historical Society, recognized the value of Austen's negatives languishing in the basement. He tried unsuccessfully to sell them to newspapers and museums, but in 1950, the year Austen was committed to the poorhouse, he received a letter from Oliver Jensen, a young editor and writer, inquiring about historic photos for a book. Brinley saw his chance. When Jensen looked at the old glass plates, he knew he had found a treasure.

Alice's life improved. Jensen had some of the photos published in *Life* and other glossy publications, earning enough to pay for Austen's removal to a private nursing home. On 9 October 1951, the Staten Island Historical Society held an "Alice Austen Day." Eighty-five-year-old Alice, wearing a large orchid and a handmade lace collar, arrived in her wheelchair to enjoy the company of 300 well-wishers. Alfred Eisenstaedt photographed her for *Life*. She was taken to visit "Clear Comfort," by then devoid of paint and inhabited by strangers. Seeing the weedy, overgrown garden she had once tended so carefully, she wept. A year later, Alice Austen died, sitting in her wheelchair on the porch of the nursing home. Today, she is better known than she ever was during her lifetime.

After Alice Austen and Gertrude Tate were evicted, "Clear Comfort" deteriorated until threatened with destruction. Preservationists managed to save both the house and grounds, which the City purchased in 1975 and restored a decade later using Austen's photos as guidelines.

JACQUES MARCHAIS & THE MUSEUM OF TIBETAN ART

Halfway up Lighthouse Hill stands the Jacques Marchais Museum of Tibetan Art (*map p. 261, D4*), the realization in stone and mortar of its founder's spiritual quest. Jacques Marchais—actress, wife, mother, art collector, dealer, and lifetime spiritual seeker—gathered some 3,000 pieces of Tibetan art during the 1930s and 1940s and then created an appropriate setting for the collection, which she valued for both religious and aesthetic reasons. An aura of unworldly serenity surrounds the place, whose rustic fieldstone buildings recreate the Buddhist monasteries of the Himalayas.

Though her achievements are concrete and visible, Jacques Marchais herself remains elusive, mainly because she wanted to be. She called herself by different names at different times in her life; she doled out contradictory autobiographical tidbits; she altered facts and dates to suit her purposes. But though she seems to have been intent on crafting a background for herself consistent with her ambitions, she did follow her beliefs sincerely and passionately.

She was born on 30 September 1887, in Cincinnati, Ohio. Thereafter her biography gets murky, beginning with her birth name. Was she Edna Coblentz? Or Jacques Marchais Coblentz? She vehemently asserted herself to be Jacques Marchais and embroidered a genealogy. On the paternal side, she said, she was related to a Jacques, a Marchais, and a sculptor. Her father, John Coblentz, died when she was younger than three, she said, and her mother put her on the stage as a toddler, renaming her "Edna." On her mother's side she was descended from the elite Philadelphia Rittenhouse family and, further back, from a knighted British sea captain active in the China trade, Sir John Norman.

Official documents—her son's birth certificate, her father's death certificate, and her first marriage certificate, and census listings—contradict this version. She was born Edna Coblentz; her father died when she was eight, though according to family members he had already abandoned Edna and her mother for a younger woman; Edna's mother took her to Chicago and left her for a while at a convent before putting her to work on the stage; the two lived in a boarding house; Edna's mother was a housekeeper, unemployed in 1900. "Edna" had become "Jacques Marchais" in the 1920 New York City census. Her outpouring of disinformation suggests that the adult Jacques Marchais hungered for a happier, more illustrious childhood than the one life had provided. In her maturity, Marchais admitted she was given to play acting and perhaps she came to believe the fictions she spun.

What she lacked in pedigree, Edna made up for in talent and drive. She appeared professionally in Chicago and as a sixteen-year-old, playing in a comedy in Boston, she met her first husband, Brookings Montgomery, a college student, son of a prominent St. Louis family. On the marriage license both bride and groom fudged their ages: she was actually 16, he was 20; but they backdated their birthdates making him 21 and her 20. The Montgomerys disinherited their son, but when the young couple found themselves financially strapped, they and their three children moved in with his parents (it can't have been easy). Not surprisingly, they divorced in 1910. Leaving the children behind, Edna returned to the stage.

Around 1916, Edna, by this time calling herself Jacqueline or Jacquie (but not yet Marchais), turned up in Greenwich Village, where the bohemian, free-floating spiritualism of the time spoke to her needs. She fell in with an artistic circle—an architect, an occultist, and an Indian classical dancer, who had begun her career performing in a dime museum. Jacques Marchais was not beautiful, but her energy attracted friends and admirers. After a brief second marriage, Marchais married Harry Klauber, the Brooklyn-born owner of a profitable chemical company. The couple moved to leafy, rural Staten Island and built a house next door to the site of the present museum. She brought her children to live with them, though their relationship was never especially good. Clearly she had more important things to do.

The Gallery and the Temple

In 1938, she opened the Jacques Marchais Gallery on East Fifty-first Street in Manhattan, buying and selling Asian art, using the profits as well as money from her husband to bankroll her projected Tibetan spiritual center. Marchais claimed her interest in Asian art had awakened when, as a child, she found in an old trunk some mysterious Tibetan figurines, brought by her grandfather from Darjeeling; she played with them as if they were dolls. But art historian Barbara Lipton, who catalogued the Marchais collection in 1996, dated the sculptures from c. 1935, when Marchais was forty-eight. Whatever the truth, her timing was good. Tibetan art was coming on the market for the first time in many years, and she picked up good pieces at good prices. Unfortunately, she was a haphazard record keeper and so the provenance of many works in her collection is unknown. The gallery remained in business until she died.

In 1941, Marchais and her husband broke ground for the Tibetan center. She drew up the plans for the buildings, disdaining professional help and instead poring over scholarly articles and photos. The City buildings' department stipulated that plans be submitted by an architect, a requirement that got her dander up: she was irate that she had to turn over *her* blueprints to the architects; *she* knew what she wanted; *she* understood Tibetan architecture; *she* had design talent and a passion for authenticity and perfection. The Tibetan center continued to be more or less a one-woman effort. She designed the buildings and the terraced gardens; she supervised construction. Working with Joseph Primiano, a local stonemason, she drove around in her Lincoln Continental, a cart attached, prospecting for stones, which she (and the Lincoln) hauled up the hill.

Her independence and self-confidence suggest a forceful, demanding personality. Though she considered herself spiritual, she drove a hard bargain and was relentless in protecting and exercising what she considered her rights; charming sometimes, she was also erratic, moody, and quick to anger. Marchais believed in religious and racial tolerance, in *karma*, and in re-incarnation; she hoped for world peace. Distressed by the bloodshed of two world wars and the economic ravages of the Depression, she envisioned her center as a respite from the anxieties of modern life.

On 5 October 1947, friends and associates witnessed the opening of the museum—an open rectangular space with a triple-tiered stone altar. She called it a "chanting hall." *Life* magazine covered the event, and in its December 5 issue published a photo of Mme Marchais wearing a long gown, her hair combed up into an impressive pompadour, standing before a bank of spinning prayer wheels that she herself had constructed. Another photo depicted her enthroned on a red Chinese lacquer chair flanked by carved lions. It must have been a proud day for Marchais, but the *Life* article, headlined "New York Lamasery: a new Tibetan temple bewilders Staten Island," exudes condescension toward the strange shrine stuffed with art objects, open for "meditation," a form of reflection barely recognized in 1947.

Unfortunately Jacques Marchais died a little more than four months after the museum opened, leaving everything to her husband. Klauber himself died seven months later, entrusting the land, buildings, collections, and a small endowment to a neighbor, Helen A. Watkins. Relatives contested the will, whose legal defense largely consumed the endowment. Helen Watkins, though well meaning, was untrained as a preservationist or a curator and over the years many pieces deteriorated or disappeared—were stolen, sold, or became victims of misadministration. Today the collection has about 1,200 pieces of art from Tibet, China, and Mongolia, dating from the fifteenth to the nineteenth centuries: bronze Buddhas, *thangkas*, Chinese cloisonné, and ceremonial objects used in Tibetan monasteries. Though the collection is small, Marchais's achievement remains remarkable.

STATEN ISLAND SAINTS

Probably the most famous women in Staten Island history are Elizabeth Ann Seton (1774–1821), canonized in 1975, and Dorothy Day (1897–1980), anarchist, pacifist, and co-founder of the Catholic Worker movement, presently on the shortlist for sainthood. Day lived for a while in the bungalow colony at Spanish Camp, which was demolished in 2001 to make way for a development of neo-mansions (still mostly unbuilt). She is buried in the Cemetery of the Resurrection (also the resting place of several reputed mobsters; *map p. 262, B6*).

St. Elizabeth Ann was the first American-born saint, founder of America's first free Catholic School, and of the Sisters of Charity, an order dedicated to caring for the children of the poor. Her father was Richard Bayley, who was for a while Chief Health Officer of the Port of New York. Her mother was daughter of the rector of St. Andrew's Church in Richmondtown. Mother Seton's name is enshrined in the former Bayley-Seton Hospital (*see p. 34*) on Vanderbilt Avenue, but there are also shrines for her in Manhattan and Maryland.

THE VANDERBILTS ON STATEN ISLAND

In 1715, a farmer of Dutch heritage packed up his earthly possessions and moved from the fields of Flatbush, Brooklyn, to sparsely settled Staten Island. The distance was less than fifteen miles as the crow flies, but the move was auspicious, not so much for Jacob Van der Bilt himself, but for his great grandson, Cornelius Vanderbilt (1794–1877), who would become one of the richest and most powerful men of his generation. Had Cornelius been born landlocked in Flatbush, his future would surely have been different. Instead he was born on the northern shore of Staten Island, a stone's throw from the water and about five miles from New York City.

Cornelius would be known as the Commodore, and his career would take him far from Staten Island, first to the waters that separated it from New York and New Jersey, then up the Hudson River, along Long Island Sound, down the New Jersey coast, eventually to the isthmus of Nicaragua and up the coast of California, and across the Atlantic Ocean. At the opportune moment, he would move his ventures from ships to railroad trains. Along the way he would amass a stupendous fortune and change the landscape of American industry. Though he died in New York City, a more fitting arena for his outsize ambitions than Staten Island, he never cut his ties to his birthplace, where he would return to be buried. In 1877, at the time of his death, Cornelius and his son William owned hundreds of acres on the Island; they controlled its access to major markets, and they impacted its entire economy.

During the eighteenth century, the descendants of Jacob Van der Bilt dispersed across the Island; most of the men worked as farmers, fishermen, or oystermen, but a few tried tavern keeping or shoe making. Many of the women produced sizeable broods, often nine or ten children. The Commodore's father, also named Cornelius Vanderbilt (1764–1832), settled on a small farm in Port Richmond. (The site of the original homestead is thought to be near Faber Park, on Richmond Terrace, between Sharpe Ave and Faber St; *map p. 260, C1*).

In 1787, he married Phebe Hand, a woman of English descent who nonetheless exemplified the Dutch virtues of frugality, industry, and shrewdness. She sold vegetables, loaned out money at interest, and even foreclosed on her widowed daughter's mortgage. The elder Cornelius supplemented his farming income as a ferryman, owning a periauger, transporting livestock and produce as well as passengers. Phebe seems to have transmitted her head for business to her second son, Cornelius.

With the birth of children, the family moved east from Port Richmond to a larger home close to the water in what became Stapleton (near 560 Bay St, where the empty Paramount Theater now stands). Cornelius grew up here, close to the Narrows, with New York City visible across the bay, near and yet far, a city inspired by commercial appetites foreign to agrarian Staten Island, "belted round by wharves…commerce [surrounding] it with her surf," as Herman Melville's Ishmael in *Moby-Dick* describes it.

Commerce drew Cornelius to the water. He was operating a ferry to Manhattan by 1811 or 1812; in 1814, he left Staten Island and moved to Manhattan, where he would come to dominate the nation's transportation industries. He left his huge fortune, mostly intact, to his son, William Henry Vanderbilt. William doubled it, but divided his estate among several children. The third and subsequent generations spent lavishly on mansions (in Manhattan, Newport, North Carolina), yachts, horses, and other ephemera, sometimes selling land to support their opulent tastes. Consequently the Vanderbilts have left few traces on Staten Island: in Port Richmond, the possible site of Cornelius's birthplace; in Clifton, Vanderbilt Avenue, which cuts seaward through former Vanderbilt land but is not a major thoroughfare. Vanderbilt Landing, where the Commodore's ferry docked, stood more or less on the site of the Clifton railroad station. A catering hall, The Vanderbilt at South Beach, hosts weddings and parties, but is related to the family in name only. The landmarked home (1836) of Cornelius's cousin, John King Vanderbilt, a grocer, stands empty and alone at 1197 Clove Rd, marooned among rows of town houses. Miller Field (*map p. 261, E4*), once a small part of William Henry's 350-acre farm, became an airfield and is now a park.

Many of Cornelius's direct descendants are interred in the Vanderbilt Mausoleum, in the Moravian Cemetery.

The Vanderbilt Mausoleum

At the northern edge of the Moravian Cemetery, in a 22-acre private plot, stands the Vanderbilt Mausoleum (*map p. 261, D3*). Like other remnants of the family's presence on Staten Island, their burial place has suffered at the hands of time, though it was intended to preserve until Judgment Day the earthly remains of Vanderbilt males directly descended from the Commodore as well as his unmarried daughters, who still bore the name of the paterfamilias. Less worthily named relatives—married daughters, their husbands and children—lie outside the mausoleum in the surrounding private park.

William Henry Vanderbilt, the Commodore's eldest son and the driving force behind the massive vault, was perhaps moved to create it by the sensational body snatching of A.T. Stewart, New York's first "merchant prince," whose remains were held for ransom. Stewart, a man with a propensity for showmanship, had made his fortune as a retailer of dry goods. His stores were lavish and his home was so opulent that it virtually put him on a footing with royalty.

Stewart died and was buried modestly, even carelessly, in the cemetery at St. Mark's Church in-the-Bowery. The kidnapping, about a month after his death in 1876, alerted other wealthy families to the possibility of a similar fate befalling the remains of their own loved ones. And so, in December 1884, William H. Vanderbilt, then in his sixties and possibly contemplating his own mortality, undertook the construction of an inviolable mausoleum. Not a moment too soon, as it turned out, since William H. died unexpectedly, before the work was completed.

William H. commissioned Richard Morris Hunt, the preferred architect of the younger Vanderbilts, to design the place. Hunt's first proposal was too fancy. The Vanderbilts, William insisted, were unostentatious people, who shunned gaudy display, at least after death. What he wanted was something "roomy and solid and rich."

And that is what he got—a mausoleum modeled on the Chapel of Saint-Gilles-du-Gard near Arles in France, its landscaping and approach road planned by Frederick Law Olmsted (*see p. 105*), who had met William H. several decades earlier in the Staten Island Agricultural Society. Olmsted sited the mausoleum magnificently, overlooking Vanderbilt farmlands and the harbor where the Commodore began his career. The rear of the building was dug into the hill, in part to keep the interior from freezing and in part because, covered by earth, it remained within the tradition of Christian burial. Vents in the façade and openings in the cupolas allowed air to circulate; channels cut in the stone exterior facilitated drainage. Stone carvings inside and out foretold heavenly bliss.

Contemporary accounts describe the mausoleum as a veritable fortress, its masonry built to withstand the extremes of climate and the assaults of most determined grave robbers. The granite walls were eight feet thick; the doors-within-doors were strongly secured. When the remains of William H. were taken to the mausoleum, the coffin was guarded by a covey of armed detectives, who then stationed themselves at the mausoleum and were seen long after the mourners had departed, pacing back and forth before the tomb like the honor guard at the Tomb of the Unknown Soldier. Or so reported the *New York Times.*

Olmsted re-sculpted the surrounding landscape just as he had reshaped a wretched patch of Manhattan into Central Park. He piled 221,755 cubic feet of earth around and over the tomb and used another 600,000 cubic feet to re-form the hills. He laid out a curved roadway that created a stunning first view of the tomb and then graded it so that horses could pull casket-laden hearses and carriages bearing mourners up the steep hill. He designed an imposing stone arch to separate the Vanderbilt plot from the rest of the cemetery and edged the access road with hedges, ferns, and evergreens. He planted some fifty varieties of trees and shrubs, including copper beeches, maples, dogwoods, elms, and Russian olive trees.

The mausoleum, unfortunately, has long been a target for vandals. In 1936, two would-be grave robbers allegedly looking for jewelry managed to hack through the bronze locks of the entrance, but were thwarted by the inner gates. Beer drinkers littered the grounds with cans and bottles. Graffitists spray-painted the walls and motorized vandals once tried to ram a truck through the doors.

Because of these assaults, the original doors were replaced by steel and the windows of the cupolas cemented in. Major storms have wrought havoc with Olmsted's landscape. And while all things mortal are affected by time, the Vanderbilt family has organized major cleanups of the property, and the Mausoleum itself is said to be in good condition, considering its age of 130 years.

THE STATEN ISLAND BLUEBELT

The Bluebelt is a system for managing storm water that uses wetlands to control runoff. In the 1970s, during the post-Bridge period of rapid development, housing construction outran the City's ability to provide sewers, both for sanitation and storm water control. During heavy rains, low-lying neighborhoods flooded and residential septic systems overflowed. In the early 1990s, the City began buying land for a Bluebelt system.

Natural wetlands store and convey water and also filter out contaminants. Today's Bluebelt attempts to recreate the Island's wetlands as they existed before heavy development. Currently the system drains sixteen watersheds (a combined area of approximately 10,000 acres) and because the program has been successful both environmentally and economically, the City seeks to expand it.

THE BRIDGES OF RICHMOND COUNTY

Arthur Kill Lift Bridge—Goethals Bridge—Outerbridge Cross-ing—Bayonne Bridge—Verrazano-Narrows Bridge

Five bridges connect Staten Island to the rest of the United States. Four cross the kills from the Island to New Jersey; the fifth sweeps across the Narrows to Brooklyn. Two of these structures, the Bayonne and the Verrazano-Narrows Bridges, designed by Othmar Ammann, are beautiful; the others are not, but all have influenced the Island's demography.

THE NEW JERSEY BRIDGES

Geographically speaking, Staten Island and New Jersey belong together, divided by the shallow waters of the Arthur Kill and Kill van Kull. Even in colonial days, ferries crossed the kills to Bayonne, Elizabethtown, and Perth Amboy. When the Port Authority of New York was created in 1921 to oversee interstate transportation, it envisioned the New Jersey–Staten Island bridges as part of a grand circumferential loop that would link New York with the mainland rail and road systems that led to the hinterlands.

The Arthur Kill Lift Bridge

This was Staten Island's first bridge (*map p. 6, A2*), built in

1886 by the Baltimore & Ohio Railroad when the B & O was competing against the stronger Pennsylvania Railroad to establish a beachhead in New York harbor. The original swing bridge with a steam-powered movable span pivoted on a clunky central masonry pier. In 1959, the present lift span replaced it, painted blue, the heraldic color of the B & O, whose luxury passenger service was the "Royal Blue."

Soon after the new bridge opened, industry began departing Staten Island: Bethlehem Steel (1960), United States Gypsum (1972), the United States Lines-Howland Hook Marine Terminal (1986), and finally Procter & Gamble (1991). Rail traffic over the bridge declined and between 1990 and 2006, it stood empty. Today the rejuvenated Arthur Kill Lift Bridge carries garbage and containerized cargo, sparing the nearby Goethals Bridge an estimated 90,000 truckloads of trash annually.

Goethals Bridge and the Outerbridge Crossing

Two almost identical trussed cantilever bridges designed by John Alexander Low Waddell also span the Arthur Kill, both planned by the Port Authority as part of the circumferential road system.

Though largely forgotten today, Waddell was a civil engineer of high repute, an inventor, a prolific speaker and writer, a dedicated educator, and a savvy self-promoter. When it came to steel-truss bridge design and construction he was among the best, leaving as his legacy more than a thousand bridges worldwide. In addition, Waddell excelled at whist, big-game hunting, and fishing. A photo taken in his later years shows a portly man with a big, drooping moustache, and two white curls framing his forehead like the scrolls on an Ionic column. Bejeweled medals from grateful governments adorn the broad expanse of his jacket. Given his outsized personality and his sterling reputation, it is not surprising that the newly-hatched Port of New York Authority chose him as lead designer for its first projects, reasoning that Waddell's name would enhance the sale of the bonds to finance them.

The central spans of both the Outerbridge and the Goethals bridges, approximately 140 feet above the water, are approached by long viaducts. Each carries nearly 30 million vehicles a year.

The **Goethals Bridge** (*map p. 6, A2*), which connects the industrial north shore of Staten Island at Howland Hook with industrial New Jersey at Elizabethport, bears the name of George Washington Goethals, chief engineer of the Panama Canal and later a Port Authority consulting engineer, who died shortly before the bridge opened. The increased size of container ships has made it obsolescent and it is slated to be replaced. The **Outerbridge Crossing** (*map p. 6, A3*), the more southerly of the two bridges, is often mistakenly referred to as the "outer bridge"—adjective, noun—as in, "Should we take the Goethals or the Outer Bridge?" While the name "Outerbridge Crossing" conjures exotic journeys, its origins are pedestrian. Eugenius Harvey Outerbridge was first chairman of the Port Authority; "crossing" avoids the redundant "Outerbridge Bridge." Outerbridge made his fortune producing a sound-absorbing fiberboard, similar to papier-mâché, used for the interior roofs of Nashes, Buicks, Studebakers, and the roadbeds of model trains. He lived on Staten Island, where his sister Mary introduced lawn tennis to the US.

Both bridges opened at 5am on 29 June 1928, an event celebrated a week earlier with bands, banners, Boy Scouts, and self-congratulatory speeches by politicians. Although Staten Island boosters and real estate interests predicted little less than a revolution, businesses and residents did not arrive in droves. Not for nearly forty years.

The Bayonne Bridge

Swiss-born Othmar H. Ammann was one of the greats, an engineering genius, an artist in steel. Modest, reserved, and orderly, he had a tireless work ethic, a designer's eye, and consummate managerial skills. His career developed slowly. For decades he assisted others, overseeing operations on their major projects and helping with design, while remaining relatively obscure. When he was in his mid-forties, the George Washington Bridge (1931) brought him fame and broadened his opportunities. It was his masterpiece, he said, but the Bayonne Bridge (*map p. 6, B2*) was the first project that was truly his own.

Ammann initially sketched the Bayonne Bridge as a suspension bridge, but when the Port Authority decided it should be capable of carrying rail as well as vehicular traffic, he redesigned it as an arch. It resembles the Hell Gate railroad bridge on which Ammann had assisted Gustav Lindenthal, considered the master bridge builder of his era, though the Bayonne is longer, lighter, and more graceful. It opened on 15 November 1931, celebrated by bands, bunting, and the usual political hoopla.

Its long viaducts rise and fall over the marshland at a constant four percent grade so that the roadway clears the water by 151 feet at mean high tide, deemed more than adequate at the time. The *New York Times* called it "impressive and haunting," and the American Society of Civil Engineers awarded it the prize for most beautiful bridge of 1931. Today this bridge, too, has become outmoded, its clearance too low for the towering container ships that maneuver through the shallow waters of the Kill van Kull. The Port Authority plans to raise the roadway 64 feet while maintaining the original arch structure, probably to the detriment of Ammann's lyrical design.

THE VERRAZANO-NARROWS BRIDGE

Though Othmar Ammann considered the George Washington Bridge his crowning achievement, other people have bestowed that honor on the Verrazano-Narrows Bridge (*map p. 6, C2*), whose very location across the mouth of New York harbor gives it stunning prominence. When it opened on 21 November 1964, it was the world's longest suspension bridge, 60 feet longer than the Golden Gate in San Francisco (today it is the ninth longest).

The dream of spanning New York bay dates back to the nineteenth century when the B & O Railroad proposed a tunnel under the Narrows to close the link opened by the Arthur Kill Bridge, but politics and financial difficulties scotched the plan before a single spadeful of dirt was turned. In 1910, one Charles Worthington, a New York engineer, designed an arch bridge to rise 260 feet above mean high tide, but that plan, too, was shelved. In the early 1920s, Mayor John Hylan revived the notion of a tunnel. Crews dug shafts in Bay Ridge, Brooklyn, and near Fort Wadsworth on Staten Island. Again the realities defeated the dreams, and the two shafts today are known as "Hylan's Holes." Bridge engineer David Steinman proposed a suspension bridge, but the economic setbacks of the Depression and the spectacular collapse of the Tacoma-Narrows Bridge in 1940 scuttled that plan.

Yet the idea of a Narrows crossing lived on. Since at least the 1930s, Robert Moses (*see p. 11*) had considered a Narrows bridge crucial to an interstate highway system that would stretch from Maine to Florida. As chairman of the Triborough Bridge and Tunnel Authority, which controlled intrastate bridges and tunnels, his power was virtually unassailable. The TBTA hired Ammann & Whitney as consulting engineers; the design team went officially to work in 1948. Construction, which began in 1959, took five years. When the bridge opened, Ammann was eighty-five years old.

The Verrazano is immense. It is slightly less than four times the weight of the Empire State Building; its clear span of 6,690 feet is almost twice that of the George Washington Bridge (3,500 feet); the 38,290 tons of galvanized steel wire in the cables could encircle the earth about six times; the towers reach some seventy stories above the water. And yet for all its size, the bridge appears light; for all its complexity it appears simple, "a triumph of simplicity, and of restraint over exuberance," said Moses, who orchestrated and starred in the ribbon-cutting ceremonies.

In general, the dedication was a whooping success. Five dignitaries snipped the ceremonial ribbon with five pairs of golden scissors; bands blared, flags flapped, and fireboats sprayed the air as ships beneath the span sounded their horns. A few people, however, were disappointed, notably some Brooklyn teenagers, unhappy that the bridge had no pedestrian walkway. "Are feet obsolete?" read one of the signs carried by a picketer. And the twelve thousand iron workers who had put the bridge together piece by piece decided, in lieu of a celebration, to attend a Mass for the three men who had died during construction.

Yet though almost everyone agreed that the bridge itself was, in the words of President Lyndon B. Johnson, "a structure of breath-taking beauty and super engineering," disagreement surrounded the choice of the name. Robert Moses, for one, disliked "Verrazano-Narrows" as too long to remember and too hard to spell; besides, he said to the head of the Italian Historical Society of America (a group lobbying for the present name), he had never heard of Verrazano. Staten Islanders polled about their preferences preferred "Staten Island Bridge," or "Narrows Bridge." The head of the Chamber of Commerce grumbled that soon people would be renaming the Hudson River, but Governor Nelson Rockefeller signed a bill into law on 9 March 1960 guaranteeing that Verrazano's name would be mentioned daily by Staten Islanders.

Ammann rode in the eighteenth of the fifty-two limousines that rolled up to the bridge for the ceremony and sat in the second row of the grandstand. Moses asked him to stand and be recognized, calling him perhaps the greatest bridge engineer of all time, but nonetheless forgetting to mention the great man's name. Ammann stood, removed his hat, acknowledged the applause, and sat down again. He was, to the end, a modest man.

The bridge had a huge impact on Staten Island. Although the pace of development began as a trickle, by the mid-1990s it had become a flood. The Island's rural atmosphere faded. The population boomed. Rows of housing, attached and semi-detached, replaced the rows of fruits and vegetables formerly tended by Greek- and Italian American truck farmers; commercial development overwhelmed small town life. The Staten Island of yesterday was fast on its way to becoming the Staten Island of today.

MILITARY STATEN ISLAND

The Struggle for Settlement—The Revolutionary War—The Civil War—Fort Wadsworth—World War II: Miller Field

Almost as soon as news of Henry Hudson's discoveries got back to Holland, the sturdily commercial Dutch began colonizing New Netherland, and by 1626 two hundred hardy souls were struggling to maintain a foothold in New Amsterdam on the southern tip of Manhattan. Some of the directors of the Dutch West India Company, who had footed the bill for Hudson's trans-Atlantic trip, applied for and received patroonships, huge land grants that required settlement of the territory. In 1630, Michael Pauw got Staten Island and part of New Jersey; Pauw built a house in what is now Jersey City, but lost money on his various ventures, fought with the Indians, and sold back his rights in 1637. The earliest battles on Staten Island were waged between the Lenape—the Native Americans who were there already—and the newly-arriving Dutch.

David Pietersen de Vries, a ship captain, received land rights in 1639 and with a few families established a farming colony near present-day Tompkinsville, but in the summer of 1641, the Lenape destroyed the plantation. A string of incidents known as the Pig War began when the Lenape allegedly killed some hogs on De Vries's land.

The governor of New Netherland, Willem Kieft, a man frequently goaded to action by his ill-controlled anger, sent soldiers to exact revenge. They killed several of the Lenape and tortured the sachem's brother. The Indians exacted swift retribution, killing four of the settlers and burning down the farm buildings. De Vries later alleged that the soldiers, not the Indians, had killed his swine, but by the next winter the cycle of revenge had escalated and spread beyond Staten Island.

In 1642, Cornelis Melyn, an Antwerp merchant, was granted all of Staten Island except what had been given to De Vries. He landed about forty settlers, perhaps at a site about a mile south of present-day Fort Wadsworth, and worked hard at establishing a colony, stinting neither money nor labor, according to his own testimony. Melyn was also authorized by director Kieft to set up a distillery and a tannery, but in the face of an Indian attack in 1643—one incident in a wider spate of killings called the Whiskey War—Melyn abandoned his colony. The next series of murders and reprisals came in 1655, when a Dutch farmer on Manhattan murdered an Indian woman for taking peaches from his trees; once again the Indians exacted swift and widespread revenge (this time the bloodshed was called the Peach War) and once again the Dutch abandoned the settlement. The slaughter took several thousand lives, most of them Native American. All three of the early Dutch attempts to colonize Staten Island had come to nothing.

Finally, six years later, Staten Island's first permanent settlement, consisting of a few Dutch, Walloon, and Huguenot families, took root at Old Dorp (today's South Beach; *map p. 261, F3*), authorized by Peter Stuyvesant.

Natives and newcomers

The cultural underpinnings of Lenape society were utterly foreign to the European arrivals. The Indians did not "own" land—they merely had the right to use it, for fishing, hunting, or agriculture—and since they did not own it, they could not sell it or trade it away by treaty. Thus the kinds of land-based social hierarchies familiar to the European settlers did not exist in Lenape society, whose social structure was matrilineal, based on kinship rather than class. Furthermore, Lenape society was nomadic; groups moved around seasonally, fishing and planting near the coastlines during the warm months, heading inland where the hunting was better during the winter. (On Staten Island, campsites and planting grounds have been discovered not only near Tottenville, but also at Fresh Kills, Great Kills, Prince's Bay, and along the Kill van Kull.) Lenape agriculture, whose work was performed mostly by women, appeared primitive to the newcomers; the Indians cleared land by slashing and burning, and they turned the soil with hand tools since they had no domesticated animals. In general, the colonists found the natives to be savages (*wilden*, as the Dutch called them), uncivilized, and poor. On the other hand, some observers were more sympathetic. According to the Reverend Charles Wolley, who lived in the colonies in 1678–80, the natives were "straight bodied" and "strongly composed," none of them "shap'd either in redundance or defect, deformed or mishapen." They were remarkably skillful with bow and arrow, so much so that a boy of seven could shoot a bird on the wing. And since they had been given access to guns, Wolley continues, they turned out to be superb marksmen "and more dangerous too" than the Europeans who had provided them with firearms.

The introduction of European culture as well as the escalating requirements of the colonists for land spelled the end for the Lenape. Diseases new to the Indians, especially smallpox and measles for which they had no resistance, decimated them. "Fire water" as well as firearms, contributed to the loss of the old ways. And while at first some of the Native Americans may have been reluctant to trade, European goods—particularly guns and alcohol—proved distressingly seductive. Disputes with the Dutch and then the British over land ownership, and wars among different groups of Native Americans, notably the Iroquois, eventually drove the Lenape westward. In 1670, the Indians signed over their last land rights to the British, and most of them left thereafter, though a few remained in small family groups, settling inconspicuously in the back acres of Dutch and British farmsteads.

The last Native Americans said to remain on Staten Island were an elderly couple, Sam and Hannah, and their daughter Nance, who lived near Fresh Kills and crafted baskets. According to historian Ira K. Morris, writing in 1898, Sam died in 1826, older than ninety years old. Nance, also according to Morris, died in the poorhouse and was buried near her father at the cemetery of the old French Church (the graveyard no longer exists).

NATIVE AMERICAN BURIAL GROUNDS

While there are indications of Native American burial grounds in several waterside locations on Staten Island, one of the most extensive such grounds on the eastern seaboard is at Ward's Point at the Island's southern tip (*map p. 6, A3*). Here the Lenape lived, camped, fished, and hunted. Here also they buried their dead. Their religion did include belief in a spiritual afterlife that reflected earthly goodness or its lack. William Penn, the first to comment on the tribe, remarked in a letter of 1683, that they believed in a "king" who made them, and that the souls of the virtuous will live again with him in a glorious country somewhere to the south.

The dead were simply placed in the dirt, though sometimes the graves were lined with grass mats. Most of the bodies were buried sitting up with flexed knees. Sometimes the hands were ceremonially folded over the chest or face. Sometimes the dead were accompanied by grave goods: deer bones (occasionally cracked to extract the marrow probably consumed at the funeral feast), axes, turtle shells, pot shards, projectile points, net sinkers, beaver teeth, and shells—lots of them. In fact, the presence of shells often served as a clue to good digging sites. Some of the skeletons bore signs of violence: a couple of crushed skulls; a skull grooved with probable tomahawk blows; an iron knife blade inserted between ribs, this last surely from colonial days.

Little marked the graves, some of which held more than one skeleton buried double-decker, but generally archaeologists have found few indications of the pre-eminence of one person over another. Most remarkable is the body of a child, about six years old, first discovered in 1895. Buried face up, head toward the east, the body was surrounded by unusually fine objects: a stone pipe, implements of jasper, a copper ornament placed over the face, a chunk of mica under the lower jaw, a necklace of white shell beads, a receptacle for paint made from the jaw of a lynx, and, richest of all, a large smoky quartz crystal, perhaps a talisman to protect the dead child from evil spirits. Many of these things came from far away and are not found in other graves in the region. The hundreds of shell beads in the necklace, for example, come from a species found in warmer coastal waters—only as far north as Virginia. Archaeologists can only guess how the child died, why such valuables were put in the grave, and how they got to Ward's Point.

THE REVOLUTIONARY WAR

During the Revolutionary War, Staten Island quickly fell to the British, whose fleet carrying an army commanded by General William Howe sailed into the Narrows in early July 1776. The bay resembled a forest of pine trees, bristling with masts. Nine thousand of His Majesty's army came ashore, and by the time the entire force had assembled, the invaders would number some 450 ships and 30,000 men, ten times the population of Staten Island.

Most Staten Islanders were delighted, filled "with Utmost Joy," as a captain in the Royal Marines commented, some locals expressing that joy by tossing forty pounds (weight, not value) of paper money into a bonfire. General Howe was understandably pleased and even King George III commended the Islanders for the warm reception. The Loyalist contingent, perhaps more than ninety percent of the local population, included many of the wealthiest and most prominent citizens, who remained perfectly content to continue under a British rule that had proven both pleasant and profitable. One such Loyalist was Christopher Billopp, whose family had received a large royal land grant a century before and had risen to the top of Staten Island society. Billopp enlisted in the provincial militia to provide the British with auxiliary support, accepting a commission as a lieutenant colonel. Isaac Decker, who operated a ferry on the Kill van Kull and also took an oath of loyalty to the king, estimated that as many as 500 men were ready to bear arms for the Loyalist cause, a considerable number given that the population of Staten Island on the eve of the Revolution was only 2,847 men, women, and children.

General George Washington recognized the Islanders' general hostility to rebellion, calling the Loyalists "our inveterate Enemies." John Adams went further, describing them as "unprincipled and unfeeling and unnatural."

As soon as the British troops landed, General Howe began organizing the army's main camp near the Watering Place in what is now Tompkinsville (*map p. 261, E1*). Many camped in sailcloth tents; others slept in fields, forests, or barns, though high-ranking officers were billeted in private homes. Howe himself took over the house of a former provincial official on what is now Richmond Terrace in New Brighton (*map p. 261, E1*). His men soon fortified the high ground on the North Shore, constructing earthworks in what is now St. George (Fort Hill Park was the site of Fort Knyphausen, a small redoubt named for the Hessian general Wilhelm von Knyphausen, whose mercenaries supplemented the regular British forces; *map p. 261, E1*.) The British also erected redoubts at Richmondtown and at the site of Fort Wadsworth, but these fortifications, mostly earthen, have long since disappeared.

Negotiations at the Conference House

Perhaps it was the Staten Island reception of his troops with "Utmost Joy," but General Howe continued to believe that the rebels were a small minority and that most Americans remained loyal to the king. The American army had barely escaped annihilation at the Battle of Brooklyn Heights, fleeing across the East River under cover of fog and night. Hoping that the dispirited Americans would see the handwriting on the wall, General Howe and his brother Admiral Richard Howe arranged for negotiations that would nip the nascent rebellion before it could flourish. If Congress would rescind the Declaration of Independence, the British would pardon (at least some of) those who had rebelled against the king.

Three delegates, John Adams, Benjamin Franklin, and Edward Rutledge, arrived on Staten Island from the Congress in Philadelphia, a two-day journey over rutted roads clogged with soldiers (today a drive of about ninety minutes). From Perth Amboy, they were ferried in the admiral's red-and-gilt barge across the Arthur Kill to Christopher Billopp's property at the southern tip of the Island (now Conference House; *map p. 262, A7*). General Howe met them at the dock, resplendent in the uniform of a Royal Navy flag officer. He escorted the three past an honor guard of Hessian mercenaries, who in the words of John Adams presented arms "looking fierce as ten Furies, making all the grimaces and gestures, and motions with their muskets with bayonets fixed, which, I suppose, military etiquette requires." Adams further noted that in the absence of Billopp, who was staying with his father-in-law, the house, occupied by the Hessian guard, was filthy as a stable, though in an effort at hospitality one parlor had been tidied up and the floor covered with green branches and moss. Adams found this decorative touch "not only wholesome, but romantically elegant."

After a meal of ham, mutton, tongue, and some good claret to wash it down, the negotiations began. Both of the brothers Howe felt well disposed toward the Americans, but discussion soon made it clear that the British could not recognize American independence and that the Americans would not forgo it. After three hours, the talks broke off. "They met, they talked, they parted," wrote Admiral Howe's secretary, "and now nothing remains but to fight it out against a set of the most determined hypocrites and demagogues, compiled of the refuse of the colonies, that ever were permitted by Providence to be the scourge of a country." Among the "hypocrites and demagogues" who would not be pardoned was John Adams. Had the negotiations succeeded, he would have been hanged.

The conference ended; Adams, Franklin, and Rutledge were ferried back to Perth Amboy and returned to Philadelphia; four days later, the British invaded Manhattan.

The British occupied the Billopp House throughout the war. When they left, the State of New York confiscated the property, and Billopp fled to Canada. A prominent Staten Islander who had thrown in his allegiance with the winning side, Samuel Ward, bought the property and passed it on to his son, who subdivided it for his many children. The house deteriorated and was even used briefly as a manufactory for rat poison; it has now been rescued as a historic site and restored by the Conference House Association, formed for that express purpose.

Occupied Staten Island

During the first months of the occupation things went well. Local farmers sold their produce willingly to the British, who paid in gold and silver instead of paper money; some Islanders enlisted in the British army; others worked for the occupiers, for example in the shipyards building flatboats for military transport, or providing wagons. But stranded on an island, with nothing much to do, the occupying force soon began to experience loss of morale and discipline, and tensions mounted. Supporters of the colonial army sabotaged the British whenever possible; sharpshooters fired on their boats patrolling the kills; ordinary citizens committed random acts of violence as local sentiment gradually turned against the occupiers. The soldiers retaliated, seized farm produce and terrorized the populace, Loyalist or not, with acts of arson, murder, theft, and sexual assault. Public disgust with the army became so intense that, according to Washington's general, William Livingston, the British troops were soon ill treated. Staten Islanders, who had at first welcomed them, were eventually willing "to poison them all."

When the British departed Staten Island in 1783, crowds stood on the heights facing the Narrows and cheered, or jeered. The Island had suffered—its forests felled, its livestock slaughtered, its fences and buildings burned. But it would rebound, and for the next century would remain as it was, a middle-class community of separate villages.

THE CIVIL WAR

Little is left on Staten Island to recall its role in the Civil War. Notable survivals are the forts at Fort Wadsworth and a marker in the Moravian Cemetery honoring Robert Gould Shaw, the son of prominent Staten Island abolitionists. But once again, as in the Revolution, Staten Island played a significant role.

Before the war broke out, Southern planters, many of whom brokered their cotton through the port of New York, escaped the oppressive summer heat in the North Shore resort hotels. Among more than fifty of these establishments during the period were the Planters Hotel, dating from around 1820 (*on the corner of Bay and Grant Sts*), a modest brick establishment with a long verandah facing the water, and the swankier Pavilion Hotel on Richmond Terrace near St. Peter's Place. The Pavilion, domed and porticoed, a glittering presence in Island social life, hosted such guests as singer Jenny Lind and banker Moses Taylor, who was said to be worth $70 million at the time. When the war broke out, some of the planters sequestered their families on Staten Island for the duration.

While many Islanders may have sympathized with the Southern cause, Staten Island also nurtured a core of abolitionists, headed by Sidney Howard Gay, editor of the *Anti-Slavery Standard* and managing editor of the *New York Tribune*, Horace Greeley's idealistic and abolitionist paper. George William Curtis, editor of *Harper's Magazine*, and Francis George Shaw, father of Robert Gould Shaw, were also active. The abolitionists propagandized energetically, organizing meetings, inviting well-known anti-slavery figures to speak, and distributing literature. Some, including the Gays and Curtises, are believed to have sheltered runaway slaves. Nonetheless, when the State of New York proposed an amendment to its constitution proposing suffrage for blacks, the canvass of Richmond County (Staten Island) totted up 2,350 votes against suffrage and 145 in favor. Hated by their opponents, the abolitionists lived in fear of violence.

In the military build-up after the war broke out, about a dozen army camps were set up on Staten Island for training and mustering soldiers before deployment to the front. On farms and large estates, even at a former baseball field, rows of tents whitened the land. In time, conditions inside the camps became deplorable and discipline slack. A physician in charge of Camp Scott recounted the filth, disease, and low morale of the troops. Richard M. Bayles in his 1867 *History of Staten Island* quotes the *Staten Island Gazette* on 12 November 1862:

> The Corcoran Legion has departed and who is sorry?
> Not the farmer whose hen roosts were robbed and

whose fences were carried away for camp fires—not the peaceable citizen who found his safest place to be within his own house after nightfall, nor his wife and daughters, who were insulted in broad day and jeered at in the foulest language by the ruffian soldiery—not the public officers of the County whose writs were disobeyed and who dare not arrest a man of their number unless they run the risk of having daylight let through their unfortunate bodies by bayonet thrust…

But all in all, Staten Island escaped unscathed.

FORT WADSWORTH

NB: "Fort Wadsworth" is the name of the present military reservation and also of the surrounding neighborhood. The principal fortifications are Battery Weed at the water's edge and Fort Tompkins up on the hill. Battery Weed was formerly called Fort Wadsworth and before that Fort Richmond; the present name was conferred in 1865 to honor Brigadier General Stephen Weed, killed at Gettysburg.

Fort Wadsworth (*map p. 261, F2–F3*), standing on the terminal moraine, commands high ground at the easternmost point of Staten Island, only about a mile from Brooklyn across the bay. Today the blue-green western tower of the Verrazano-Narrows Bridge overshadows the old fort and the roadway suspended overhead drones with traffic day and night. Still, you can stand on an overlook above the fort and enjoy a view that suggests why Hudson and Verrazano thought themselves almost in paradise. To the north in the far distance, the southern tip of Manhattan protrudes into the Upper Bay. To the east, sturdy Fort Hamilton hunkers down on the coast of Brooklyn just south of the bridge tower. Maritime traffic in the Narrows slides by, for the most part silently—container ships, cruise boats, tugs, tankers, occasionally a sailboat. The view of New York Harbor is panoramic; but then, that is why the fort was sited here.

Below the overlook on the Staten Island shoreline, the granite walls of Battery Weed surround a grassy parade ground. Further up the hill flanking the modern roadway stand the massive masonry walls of Fort Tompkins (on your left as you face the water) and Battery Duane (on the right). During the summer, rented goats chomp away behind electrified fences at the invasive vegetation; signs warn you not to feed them, but even these notoriously omnivorous animals can't keep up with the encroaching vines, whose tangled stems have grown as thick as your wrist.

Beginnings

Although the site was fortified in the eighteenth century, Fort Tompkins and Battery Weed as they appear today date from around the Civil War, a period of intense military construction following the War of 1812. During that war the British had landed a large army near New Orleans; they had sailed up Chesapeake Bay to Washington and burned the nation's capital; and they had successfully blockaded American cities, stifling commerce and pinning American warships in port. Clearly the country needed fortifications to keep enemy ships from entering American harbors.

The coastal fortifications built between 1817 and 1867, known as Third System fortifications, were closed structures with tall, thick masonry walls, an improvement over earlier fortresses made of brick, wood, and earth. They were equipped with smoothbore cannons that could shoot three miles, effective against the ironclad ships being constructed during the Civil War. The Narrows became a first point of defense for New York harbor.

As the prospect of war clouded the horizon, the federal government built two new forts overlooking the Narrows: Fort Richmond (Battery Weed) and Fort Tompkins. Battery Weed, constructed of granite, has three tiers whose guns were mounted in fortified chambers (casemates) with iron-shuttered gun ports, and a top tier (barbette) whose guns were fired over a chest-high parapet rather than through openings. The only entrance was across a drawbridge over a moat. The chief architect, Joseph G. Totten (incidentally, a relative of the Tottenville Tottens), created in Battery Weed a beautiful structure, described by General Philip Sheridan a couple of decades after the

Civil War as the most beautiful masonry work he had ever seen. The gun platforms were ready by 1860 for a full complement of 116 guns bearing on the Narrows plus twenty-four smaller flanking guns.

Fort Tompkins, higher on the bluff and built to protect Battery Weed, also provided living quarters for the troops who manned the batteries. Congress voted money to buy additional land for Fort Tompkins in 1851, but construction did not actually begin until 1859 and was not completed until 1876, twelve years after the Civil War had ground down to its fateful ending. By then both forts were obsolete, their masonry walls vulnerable to newer and more powerful weaponry.

Encroaching obsolescence

In 1885 and again in 1898, a government panel named for Secretary of War William C. Endicott called for upgrading coastal fortifications nationwide, replacing masonry with concrete and smoothbore guns with rifled cannons, mortars, and rapid fire artillery, far more accurate and more deadly. Endicott Period Defenses also included mining the harbor with "torpedoes" (fixed mines that were hauled into position by cables and detonated from shore) and installing submarine nets. But by the time of World War I, increasing gun ranges had reduced the effectiveness of the mine defense systems, and when the war ended the garrison of 1,400 men was reduced to a mere fourteen. Though anti-aircraft guns were installed in the 1930s, the use of aircraft and long-range missiles spelled the end for the old forts. During World War II, the military developed plans to deploy submarine mines across the Narrows from Battery Weed, but it is uncertain whether they were implemented; the base was used to house Italian prisoners of war, and in 1942, the last manned battery was taken out of service. Finally, in 1972, the Department of Defense declared Fort Wadsworth surplus property and turned it over to the National Park Service.

THE FORT WADSWORTH LIGHTHOUSE

On the northeast bastion of Battery Weed sits the Fort Wadsworth Lighthouse, the replacement for one built in 1828 on the shoreline south of the fort. The Verrazano-Narrows Bridge made the light redundant and it was abandoned. Vandals broke the windows, seagull droppings and rust took their toll, until a posse of volunteers headed by Joe Esposito restored the light; now solar-powered, the Fort Wadsworth Light was ceremonially relit in 2005.

Since 1992, Fort Wadsworth has been part of the Gateway National Recreation Area. The 226-acre reservation contains parkland as well as buildings for the armed services and other government agencies. Battery Weed and Fort Tompkins were never fired upon, but their presence as guardians of New York Harbor has been both real and symbolic.

WORLD WAR II: MILLER FIELD

In 1921, when Miller Field (*map p. 261, E4*) opened as an Army Air Corps base, it was the only coastal air defense station on the eastern seaboard. Facilities included a concrete seaplane ramp, two grass runways, three 85-foot radio masts, and four airplane hangars. The Army named the base for James Ely Miller, who had been shot down over France (the first American flyer killed in action during World War I). Before the base was deactivated in 1965, Miller Field served as a Coast Artillery gun site, an airfield for private aviators, a Nike Missile Repair Depot, and a Green Beret training base. Today Miller Field is bare and wind-swept; giant New Dorp High School occupies its southwest corner; athletic fields occupy some of its 187 acres, though a few remnants of its past still stand.

Cornelius "Commodore" Vanderbilt began buying land in the vicinity around 1839. His son, William H. Vanderbilt, was exiled to a farm here, penalized for what the Commodore considered a subpar performance with a Wall Street banking firm. William vindicated himself, doubling his inheritance, bequeathing the farm to his youngest son, George Washington Vanderbilt who, because of his birth order, was relieved of having to run the family business. A fortunate thing, because George preferred philosophy, literature, and the fine arts to steamboats and railroads. George did, however, inherit the Vanderbilt mania for building big and lavished much of his fortune on "Biltmore," a 250-room neo-chateau surrounded by hundreds of thousands of acres of North Carolina woodlands. (It was Frederick Law Olmsted who undertook its landscaping and he who suggested to Vanderbilt the creation of an arboretum and a systematically managed forest.) When George Vanderbilt died in 1914, his cash-strapped widow began selling off real estate. In 1919, the government bought the tract that became Miller Field.

During World War II, the Army installed coastal artillery and a stubby concrete tower for spotting enemy warships. It stands, defaced with graffiti and streaked with rust, two sinister horizontal slits facing seaward near the beach at the eastern edge of the park. A submarine net from Miller Field stretched across the Narrows. Troops trained here before being sent to fight in Europe and Africa.

Until November 2012, two historic structures remained at Miller Field: a double seaplane hangar from the original Army Air Corps base, and the Elm Tree Light. The Elm Tree Light is still there (see p. 89) but the seaplane hangar was damaged beyond repair by the storm surge that followed Hurricane Sandy.

On 16 December 1960, a United Airlines Douglas DC-8 and a Trans World Airlines Lockheed Super Constellation collided west of Miller Field during a snowstorm. The Constellation plunged to the ground at the northwest corner of the airport and the DC-8 flew eleven more miles, to crash in Brooklyn.

ETHNIC STATEN ISLAND

*The ethnic mix—The Victory Diner—Italian Staten Island—
Garibaldi and Meucci—Our Lady of Mount Carmel—Italian
Staten Island today: Gangsters and Guidos*

Because Staten Island remained relatively undeveloped for centuries, it has managed to retain traces of its first European settlers, the Dutch. There are seventeenth- and eighteenth-century houses in the Dutch style, several of them clustered in Historic Richmond Town; and Dutch place names—New Dorp, the Kill van Kull and other kills, Van Duzer St, and of course the name of the borough itself. The French Protestants who arrived in the seventeenth century also scattered their names about the landscape, on roads (Poillon Ave, Androvette Ave, Billiou St) and on entire communities—the neighborhoods of Huguenot and Annadale (Anna Seguine married into one of the early Huguenot families).

The British who took over Staten Island soon defined the dominant culture and the *lingua franca*. Nieuw Dorp became New Town and in 1683, Staaten Eylandt became Richmond County, named for the first Duke of Richmond, illegitimate son of Charles II. (It remained the Borough of Richmond until given its present name in 1975.)

From the early days there was also a black population, both free and slave. Although records are scarce and perhaps untrustworthy, an unofficial census in 1698 suggests that slightly less than ten percent of Staten Islanders were enslaved; according to a later government census, that figure had risen to about 22 percent in 1790. In 1799, the State of New York passed a law stating that no child could be born into slavery after 4 July 1800, and on 4 July 1827 slavery was abolished altogether in the state. According to historian Ira K. Morris, recounting in 1898 an elderly friend's recollection from seven decades earlier, Staten Island's remaining 698 slaves celebrated their emancipation for two days with singing, firecrackers, and speeches at the Swan Hotel on what is now Richmond Terrace, some of the attendees walking all the way from the southern tip of the Island, a distance of some thirteen miles.

In the nineteenth century, immigration began in earnest. Irish, Germans, and Italians arrived from the 1840s onwards, seeking relief from hunger, poverty, and political oppression. Toward the end of the century, Eastern European Jews began to come, joined by Scandinavians, some of whom found work in the shipyards along the kills. After the turn of the twentieth century, Greeks came, most of them farmers who settled around Bulls Head, New Springville, and Travis, first renting farms and later owning them. Between about 1930 and 1970, the farmers grew produce—spinach, onions, beets—which they carted to Manhattan markets. Pollution from New Jersey and escalating land prices after the opening of the Verrazano-Narrows Bridge brought about the demise of truck farming. Other Greeks started businesses in Port Richmond: dry cleaners, candy stores, shoe repair shops, and restaurants. Greek Americans have long been associated with diners, in Staten Island as elsewhere, and it is estimated that Greek immigrants founded some six hundred diners in the New York region.

THE VICTORY DINER

Staten Island's most celebrated diner was founded in 1964 on Victory Boulevard, moved to Dongan Hills, and was bought in 1982 by the Pappas family. A classic 1940s model with a décor of stainless steel, glass brick, and Formica, its streamlined railroad-car look has attracted movie directors seeking ambience, ordinary people seeking a place to unwind, and at least one couple looking for a memorable place to get married. In 2007, it was slated for demolition, but Staten Islanders stepped in, bought it, and anted up $20,000 to have it trucked to Midland Beach, where it was to have been spruced up as the centerpiece of a planned beachside park. In 2012, the torrent of water that followed Hurricane Sandy surged through it. But in preparation for the restoration, all the period details had been removed and stored: the stainless steel trim and the interior wall panels; tables; booths; and the original refrigerator. Though its steel frame was damaged, the diner may yet live again to serve up its classic burgers and fries.

Today Staten Island is New York City's whitest borough (64 percent, down from 77.6 percent in 2000). Of the white population, people of Italian heritage comprise the largest group, followed by the Irish, Germans, and Poles. The borough is home to an estimated 50,000 Jews, with the bulk of its 7,000 Russian-speaking Jews—many of whom arrived in the last twenty years—living in the Midland Beach and New Dorp neighborhoods, near the Lower Bay. Long the most homogeneous borough, the Island is becoming more diverse. Port Richmond at the northwest edge of the Island, which has the largest black population, is also a hub for Mexican immigrants. A Sri Lankan community in Tompkinsville has become one of the world's largest outside the mother country. But Italian Americans still dominate.

ITALIAN STATEN ISLAND

The predominance of Italians on Staten Island seems fitting, since the first European to set eyes on it was Giovanni da Verrazano, born south of Florence in Castello da Verrazzano (two z's; the Port Authority changed the spelling when they named the bridge). In the mid-nineteenth century a few Italian political refugees, including Giuseppe Garibaldi, lived in the northeast part of the Island, but it was not until the 1880s that immigrants came *en masse*, most of them from southern Italy, arriving via steerage. Beginning in the late 1960s a second wave arrived, Italian Americans mainly from southern Brooklyn, who reached Staten Island via the Verrazano Bridge.

Today the Italian American presence on the Island is unmistakable. There are red-sauce restaurants, pizzerias, pasticcerias, gelaterias, and Italian delis, as well as more formal restaurants with Italian menus; there are myriad small businesses—funeral homes, beauty salons—with Italian names. On lofty Grymes Hill the Casa Belvedere, an Italian cultural center, occupies a former mansion built by a wealthy German industrialist. On Todt Hill, architect Ernest Flagg's "Stone Court" (*see p. 45*) has become the home of the Center for Migration Studies, which documents the immigrant experience, especially of Italian Americans. In many neighborhoods, a flamboyant Italian American style of landscaping and holiday lighting enlivens the streetscape.

Early arrivals: Garibaldi and Meucci

Giuseppe Garibaldi (1807–82) came to Staten Island in 1850. He was swashbuckling, courageous, and charismatic, his low voice and his penetrating gaze capable of rousing men to volunteer their lives and women to surrender their hearts. His time on Staten Island was a hiatus in a career that had soared and crashed but would ascend again. The career of his contemporary, Antonio Meucci (1808–89), on the other hand, was fading. Meucci was a stage designer and technician, an inventor, and a onetime political activist who had been jailed in Italy. He had fled to Cuba, but his political past shadowed him there and he made his way to the United States, hoping to capitalize on his inventions.

Antonio Meucci was hardworking, passionate about the possibilities of electricity, and brilliant as an inventor, but unworldly. He never learned to speak English well enough to navigate the business community. And he had bad luck. He came to the US in 1850, financially comfortable, but within a decade he was poor, defrauded by investors. By 1853, his wife had become an invalid, crippled by arthritis and barely able to leave her bedroom. He was severely burned when the boilers of the Staten Island ferry, *Westfield II* (*see p. 58*), blew up in 1871.

Meucci patented processes for getting paper pulp from wood and fizzy drinks from fruit; he invented a plastic paste for molding billiard balls, vases, and statuary. In Havana, he had improved the water supply; on Staten island, he established factories for beer and candles; he developed a better (i.e. more lethal) form of ammunition, which he offered to the US Army during the Civil War and to Garibaldi. (Neither took him up on the proposal.)

But his greatest achievement was the invention of a prototype for the telephone, for which he built working models from ideas conceived as early as 1849 while he was still in Havana. Meucci filed his first patent caveat, a provisional patent application, for his telephone in 1871, by then unable to afford $250 for a full patent. While he was hospitalized after the *Westfield II* accident, his wife in financial desperation sold his original *teletrofono* models to a second-hand dealer for six dollars. The caveat had to be renewed annually, which Meucci did several times; to his lasting grief, he failed to do so in 1876, the year in which Alexander Graham Bell received his patent for the telephone; fame and riches followed, but not for Meucci.

Meucci sued. Several trials in the 1880s advanced the validity of his claims but resulted in verdicts favoring Bell. Not really surprising considering Meucci's poverty, his linguistic inadequacy, and his immigrant status. If you ask an Italian who invented the telephone, chances are you will not hear the name of Alexander Graham Bell. Meucci has at last received recognition, however, if only of the honorary kind: in 2002, the US House of Representatives passed a resolution honoring Meucci for his work on the development of the telephone and the following year the Italian government issued a stamp in his honor.

Giuseppe Garibaldi arrived in 1850, already celebrated, but fleeing Italy after the Roman republic collapsed in 1849. Hoping to raise money to buy a ship and return to his seafaring career, he lived at Meucci's small house, where the two men worked together making candles. Garibaldi hunted and fished, even writing letters complaining about the lack of big game in local woods. When funds for his own ship did not materialize, he sailed for

Central America and Peru with an Italian merchant, returning to New York briefly in 1853, then leaving for England never to return. Nonetheless, he has not been forgotten on Staten Island.

The Victorian Gothic cottage (c. 1840) where the two men lived has been opened to the public as the Garibaldi-Meucci Museum (*see p. 215*) by the Order Sons of Italy in America.

The first wave of Italian immigration

In the late nineteenth century, the first waves of Italian immigrants reached the shores of New York Bay. They were escaping *la miseria*, the hopeless rural poverty of southern Italy. For centuries, peasant families had labored in what amounted to feudal servitude, working the fields of wealthy landowners or trying to wrest a living from their own minuscule plots, divided and subdivided over the generations. *La miseria* was dominated by primitive housing, exhausted soil, deforestation, illiteracy, and illness, all cemented in place by unyielding tradition. The unification of Italy became the stimulus that impelled the poor to leave their native land, its rural poverty exacerbated because the southern provinces, controlled by an indifferent aristocracy, could not compete with the agricultural or industrialized might of the north.

Most of the immigrants were single men, laborers and agricultural workers, although some were skilled artisans—masons, mosaic workers, or plasterers. Like other immigrant groups, they stuck together, living with *paesani*, people from their home villages, clinging to the old ways, speaking the old language, distrusting outsiders. They formed mutual aid societies, which offered social opportunities, burial and life insurance, and the comfort of Old World traditions. Because their exuberant piety, sometimes tinged with anti-clericalism, made them unwelcome in the city's Irish Catholic parishes, the Italian immigrants formed their own churches and imported their own religious practices. One of the figures most venerated by the Italian immigrants is Our Lady of Mount Carmel.

Staten Island Italians settled on the North Shore, in Rosebank or West Brighton, and worked on the railroad and docks, remaining in labor-intensive jobs for decades. In the 1880s, native Staten Islanders had been bewildered by the immigrants' unintelligible language and startled by their customs—their lunches of bread and onions, their practice of dipping bread crusts into a communal pot of soup. By the 1930s, however, Italian Americans were sufficiently accepted to gain civil service positions—as construction workers on WPA projects or as sanitation men. As immigration increased, southern Italian culture became visible on Staten Island.

The Shrine of Our Lady of Mount Carmel

One of the purest remaining examples of southern Italian culture on the Island is the remarkable Shrine of Our Lady of Mount Carmel in Rosebank (*map p. 261, F2*), built by the Society of Our Lady of Mount Carmel, originally an immigrant support group.

Small houses line the sidewalks of dead-end Amity Street. Garbage cans are marshaled on the curbs. It is a streetscape of garage doors and asphalt shingles, gray and brown. And then, in midblock, is an unexpected garden, green and leafy in the summer, blooming with flowers both real and artificial. In it stands the grotto of Our Lady of Mount Carmel, patroness of the Carmelite Order, a figure so revered by New York's Italian immigrants that there are churches dedicated to her in the four other boroughs. The grotto, likened by one of the faithful to an ancient, jeweled city, is a work of imagination and reverence, a piece of folk art listed on the National Register of Historic Places. Constructed of cement embedded with thousands of small stones, marbles, bicycle reflectors, sea shells, and bits of glass, all set in orderly fashion on an architectural background of spires and turrets, pointed arches, and niches, it has a hint of Gaudí's hyperbolic *Sagrada Família* and also a tinge of Coney Island's palmier days. The central niche holds the statue of Our Lady surrounded by Mass cards, photos of loved ones, prayers scrawled on bits of paper, candles, and statuettes of saints donated by people who didn't want to throw them in the trash—so many, in fact, that one observer compared the place to a nursing home for saints.

The shrine was built over several years, by ordinary workers, some employed by the WPA during the Depression. Vito Russo (1885–1954), an immigrant from the Campania region of southwest Italy, was the moving spirit behind the project, his motivation either a vow made before he left Italy or grief for a son who died of pneumonia in 1935. The work began in 1937. Russo constructed a model in paper, cardboard, and aluminum foil, which workmen replicated with found materials—shells from the shores of the Narrows, fieldstone building blocks from WPA work sites. Sanitation workers gathered smooth round stones from along their routes and carried them home in bushel baskets. They built wooden frames in the basement of the Society meeting hall, pressed the stones and shells into sand, and then cemented them in place before carrying the frames outdoors and adding them to the shrine. Like medieval cathedrals, the grotto is a work of many people over many years, and even now remains unfinished, the manual skills of the fathers not always having been transmitted to the sons.

The feast day of Our Lady of Mount Carmel is July 16; during the week-long celebration, members of the Mount Carmel Society parade the image of the Virgin through the streets. The faithful pin money to ribbons that flutter from her hands; after the parade there is the usual feast—ice cream, *zeppole* (fried dough), sausages, Italian street food, all of it deliciously laden with fat, sugar, and salt. People come from all over the city and beyond.

ITALIAN STATEN ISLAND TODAY

When off-islanders look askance at Staten Island's Italian culture, it's not about the pizza or the gelato or the Rosebank shrine. It's about "Staten Italy," a term used both positively and negatively to suggest the Island's large Italian American population On the positive side, it is sufficiently acceptable that at least one business invoked the name—Staten Italy Bagels—and there is a web site dedicated to all the "good things Italian that come from Staten Island." Speaking negatively, "Staten Italy" is a place with real and imagined connections to organized crime and to an urban culture called "guido."

The Gangsters

The murder of Paul Castellano (1915–85), reputed *capo* of the Gambino crime family, made it impossible to deny a Staten Island-Mafia connection. At the end of his career, Castellano lived in a Todt Hill mansion at 177 Benedict Road, a seventeen-room white marble White House look-alike with a stately portico, a sweeping circular driveway, a landscaped lawn, and a swimming pool that occupied most of the back yard. Inside were marble floors, glittering chandeliers, heavy drapes, and a serious security system supplemented by a couple of Doberman pinschers. Castellano, who had become a recluse working from home, made the fatal error of arranging a dinner meeting in Manhattan. His rival John Gotti dispatched gunmen who shot

Castellano and his chauffeur-cum-heir-apparent, Tommy Bilotti (also a resident of Staten Island, but of less lofty Huguenot) in front of Sparks Steakhouse on the Upper East Side.

Castellano was a gentlemanly figure, disciplined, immaculately tailored, and generally courteous, who remained above the fray by delegating the less pleasant aspects of his job to lower-ranking assistants; he captured the public imagination and even commanded the grudging respect of the FBI agents who bugged his home. He was generous with his friends and lavish with his family, bestowing a red sports car on the live-in maid who was also his lover. Bilotti, however, was said to be violent and loutish.

After Castellano's death, the Todt Hill mansion was sold. But the demise of Paul Castellano did not mean the end of the Mafia on Staten Island, either in fact or fiction. Newspapers regularly report the doings of *mafiosi* less gentlemanly than Castellano. In 2012, a Staten Islander was charged with shaking down an employee of a Brooklyn pizzeria for stealing a recipe for tomato sauce from a family-owned Staten Island restaurant; the *New York Daily News* called the incident a "gangland sauce summit," which the UPI news agency followed up with "Ex-associate: Sauce set off mob dispute." The year before, a federal judge sympathized (slightly) with a paroled gangster who complained that he couldn't go straight because he was surrounded by mobsters: Staten Island is very small, said the parolee, and every time he went out, he met someone from his criminal past.

Staten Island's reputation for mob connections has found its way into movies, TV, and literature. Most famously, scenes from Francis Ford Coppola's *The Godfather* were filmed on the Island at a house at 110 Longfellow Ave (*map p. 261, E2*), which has become a minor drive-by tourist attraction.

The Guidos

According to the popular conception a "guido" (fem. "guidette") is a white, urban working-class male, usually but not always Italian in heritage, who lives in the New York metropolitan area, often southern Brooklyn, Staten Island, or northeastern New Jersey. (In Chicago, this person is a "Mario.") The term is usually considered an ethnic slur, though some guidos identify themselves as such and other observers dispute the negative connotations.

Guido style can include gold jewelry, spiked hair, a year-round tan, and clothing that shows off the impressive biceps, triceps, pecs and abs achieved by hours of working out in the gym. Stereotypically, guidos drive muscle cars with booming sound systems; they frequent dance clubs; they lard their conversation with Italianisms. The guido subculture imitates gangster style, though diluted and without the violent crime.

Just as guido style connotes hyper-masculinity, guidette accouterments suggest flamboyant femininity: heavy makeup especially black eyeliner, significant cleavage, short skirts, high heels, long hair, and ample jewelry. Both genders have played major roles on the TV "reality" shows *Jersey Shore* or *Mob Wives*, to the irritation of other Staten Islanders and Italian anti-defamation groups, who rightly believe that the shows give their borough and their ethnic group a bad reputation.

But guidos of both genders flaunt the style; they are flashy, independent, and deliberately outrageous.

Some academics and cultural anthropologists consider guido (the style) a "crisis of masculinity," or "a celebration of ignorance." Others say that it is simply an aspect of youth culture or a strategy for redefining a pejorative term invented by outsiders. The gold jewelry can be construed as a response to the poverty of earlier immigrant generations, the cult of the body beautiful as a flaunting of youthfulness, the Italianisms as an affirmation of ethnic identity. According to this argument, guido style provides a way to respect your heritage and yet dabble your toe in the mainstream, to thumb your nose at outsiders while confirming your own identity, to be simultaneously Italian and cool.

THE OUTCASTS OF THE ISLAND

Staten Island as refuge: The Quarantine—New York City Farm Colony—Seaview Hospital—Willowbrook

The islands of the New York archipelago have long sheltered society's unwanted. Immigrants, criminals, paralytics, the insane, the indigent, the addicted, the contagious, and, of course, the dead, have been relegated to the smaller humps of land protruding through the waters surrounding New York City. Hart Island, Riker's Island, Welfare (now Roosevelt) Island, Ellis Island—all have been refuges of first or last resort.

Staten Island, far larger than these small land masses, shares that history, influenced—as is much of the Island's past—by its longtime rural seclusion. Over the decades, philanthropists and government agencies built on its farmland a poorhouse, homes for retired mariners and orphans, way stations for the possibly contagious, and hospitals for the tubercular and the mentally ill. Some of these establishments survive, though not in their original forms nor serving their original purposes. Several of them, once beautiful, have been designated as landmarks; but in cases where financial support or alternative uses have been lacking, these abandoned places have been left, sadly, to rot and ruin. Taken together, they illustrate a chapter of Staten Island's philanthropic and institutional past that parallels the history of charity in the larger City.

THE QUARANTINE

At the end of the eighteenth century, Staten Island was still a rural county of the state. Its wide open spaces, perhaps inevitably, began to be seen as ideal repositories for those things—and people—that posed a danger or a nuisance to New York City. In 1799, the New York City Commissioners of Health requisitioned thirty acres in what is now Tompkinsville (*map p. 261, E1*) for a quarantine hospital; two years later the Quarantine was up and running.

Many immigrants who had endured long voyages in steerage, stacked in tiers of bunks below deck, the hatches closed in bad weather, the air fetid, the food foul, arrived already sick with typhus, cholera, or smallpox. The quarantined ships dropped anchor near the Tompkinsville hospital: and as the locals had feared, workers moving between the ships and the village brought home these contagious diseases.

The villagers agitated for change; nothing happened. Forty-seven years went by; a committee recommended moving the Quarantine. Another seven years passed as interest groups in New York and New Jersey bickered over its location. Finally, in 1857, the state bought land at remote Seguine Point (*map p. 262, B6*), but the locals almost immediately burned the new station down. The state moved the Quarantine back to Tompkinsville. The villagers complained again, and failing to get relief from the government, took the law into their own hands.

On 1 September 1858, a crowd of local luminaries and ordinary agitators arrived by night armed with bundles of straw, bottles of turpentine, and boxes of matches. Near the hospital wall someone had stacked heavy wooden beams with handles conveniently attached, which the attackers deployed as battering rams. After setting fire to the unoccupied buildings, the crowd cleared the men's hospital "of every living thing, even to a cat and a canary bird," according to Dr. Frederick Hollick, writing in 1893. The attackers then placed the three yellow fever patients on beds under an open shed, and burned down the hospital. The men of Tompkinsville, who had hoped that their raid would convince the authorities to move the Quarantine elsewhere, heard rumors of rebuilding, and returned on September 2 to finish what they had begun.

The state sent in the militia; the media denounced Staten Islanders as barbarians, incarnate fiends, and savages. A Richmond County judge, however, while ordering Staten Island to pay $133,822.12 in damages, exonerated the ringleaders with a ruling that modern Islanders would appreciate:

Undoubtedly the City of New York is entitled to all the protection in the matter that the State can give consistently with the health of others; she has no right to more. Her great advantages are attended by correspondent inconveniences; her great public works by great expenditures; her great foreign commerce by the infection it brings. But the Legislature can no more apportion upon the surrounding communities her dangers than her expenses; no more compel them to do her dying than to pay her taxes; neither can be done.

The Quarantine thereafter moved offshore: to hospital ships, to Hoffman and Swinburne Islands (*map p. 6, C2–C3*) to Ellis Island, and eventually to Kennedy Airport.

THE NEW YORK CITY FARM COLONY

At one time the New York City Farm Colony, the poorhouse, was a model charity, a source of philanthropic satisfaction—even pride—to Staten Islanders. Located in the neighborhood of Willowbrook, southwest of the intersection of Brielle and Walcott Avenues (*map p. 261, D3*), it encompassed some 165 acres including cultivated fields and a campus of brick and stone buildings. In 1832, there were twenty-six residents, a number that burgeoned to as many as two thousand in the early twentieth century. The "inmates," as they were then called, worked the land, their labor said to demonstrate what scientific agriculture could do with mediocre soil. Farm Colony vegetables took ribbons at the County Fair, and its produce fed not only the poor who lived in the Colony but as many as three thousand residents of other New York City institutions. A 1909 booklet describing the Colony's features points out—with some condescension—that in addition to raising fruits and vegetables, chickens and pigs, some of the inmates were instructed in basketry by a worker from the State Charities Aid Society.

Its most famous denizen, however, was no mere basket-weaver. The Colony at one time harbored the notorious Willie Sutton.

Willie Sutton: hospital orderly and bank robber

When Willie Sutton appeared at the Farm Colony, he was ranked #11 on the FBI's first "Most Wanted" list. In February 1947, he had escaped from a penitentiary in Philadelphia, hitchhiked to New York, assumed the name Eddie Lynch, and got a job as an orderly in the Farm Colony's hospital wards. Although the job paid only eighty dollars a month, it gave him room and board, enabling him to live anonymously. He found the Farm Colony congenial and the residents, whom he insisted on calling "guests" not "inmates," deserving of his compassion.

He remained there for about two years, the longest stretch of legitimate work in his lifetime. In his two somewhat conflicting autobiographies he paints himself as hardworking and kind, his single vice the compulsion to rob banks, which he claimed he was forced to do for the same reason George Mallory climbed mountains: because they were there. Sutton could not, he said, walk by a bank without mentally casing the place, even if he had no intentions of robbing it.

For his calling he was perfectly suited—skillful with his hands, intelligent, observant, and patient. Capable of meticulous planning, he was also possessed of unflappable *sang-froid* and could talk himself out of dicey situations. He didn't drink, didn't gamble, and kept his mouth shut. Well-mannered and immaculately groomed, his upper lip adorned with a pencil-thin moustache, he had only one weakness: a love of natty clothing. It led to his downfall.

Sutton's stay at the Farm Colony was an idyllic episode in a conflicted and turbulent life, half of which was played out behind bars. And yet on Staten Island, he claims, he tried to go straight, to master his insatiable urge to steal. Assigned to work in Ward 27, he mopped floors, pushed patients around in their wheelchairs, and carried their coffins to the morgue wagon. Because he could ill afford to be noticed, he said little but listened a great deal. And yet he made friends, he admired some of his co-workers and was himself respected; he felt almost safe. Sutton's stay at the Farm Colony ended in March 1950, when his landlady recognized him from a picture in the newspaper. He fled to Brooklyn and resumed his life of crime.

Less than two years later, his freedom ended. He was identified—erroneously he claimed—from a bank hold-up in Sunnyside, Queens. The police, aware of Sutton's sartorial vanity, circulated his photo to the press and also to the city's clothiers. A 24-year-old tailor's son, Arnold Schuster, recognized Sutton in the DeKalb Avenue station of the subway on 18 February 1952 and tipped off the police. Schuster paid dearly for his act. On March 8 he was gunned down near his home in Borough Park, Brooklyn. (Although the case was never definitively solved, a Mafia figure later asserted that the Gambino crime family don, Albert Anastasia, ordered the murder, because Schuster was a "squealer.") Anastasia was himself murdered in 1957. "Slick Willie," "Willie the Actor," "the Master of Crime," was sent to Atticus Prison in upstate New York. Released because of his health, he died in Florida at the age of 79.

The history of the Farm Colony

Throughout the colonial period and into the early nineteenth century, rural Staten Island had less need for public charity than more urbanized Manhattan. In general, the needy were "boarded" in their own homes or with neighbors. In other instances, strangers were paid to take in the poor. The funds for food, clothing, and shelter came primarily from churches, though in 1693 a New York state tax was approved to add public money to the coffers. This kind of support, which today would be called welfare, was known as "outdoor relief," in contrast to "indoor relief," which meant institutionalization. Those relegated to the poorhouse were people at the bottom of the heap—seriously ill, crippled or blind, very old ("ancient" in the parlance of the time), or without any ties to the surrounding community—for example sailors or travelers who had fallen suddenly ill.

Around 1700, an almshouse existed at Cocclestown (an early name for Richmondtown). Almost nothing is known about this early poorhouse, except that it was a low building in the Dutch Colonial style. In 1803, the Richmond County supervisors bought land for a "poor farm," spending $262.50 on two acres including a small-frame two- or three-room farmhouse and other outbuildings. Such reuse of existing domestic buildings as poorhouses was usual at the time, especially since attitudes toward poverty were non-punitive. Even buildings especially constructed as poorhouses looked like ordinary homes, and they accommodated the poor in domestic routines and situations—no uniforms, no marching in lockstep, no armed guards.

Soon the population of indigents outgrew the original facility, and in 1829, the county supervisors bought ninety acres and officially established the Richmond County Poor Farm at the present location. They hired (1832) a superintendent for $200 a year and a physician who got $19.50 annually for providing medical services. In the following two decades the supervisors expanded the acreage, constructed a stone dormitory, added a cholera hospital (1832), and built an asylum for the insane (1837).

But attitudes toward poverty were changing. Between 1790 and 1830, both the nation's population and the density of cities increased greatly (New York City, for example, grew from 33,131 to 202,589 during those four decades), their greater size and density destroying the former cohesion of towns, which had once solved their social problems on their own. Furthermore, the spectacle of individuals moving up and down the social scale undermined the notion of an ordered society. Once the poor had lost their status, however lowly in the hierarchy, they were seen as responsible for their own condition, and thus culpable for their poverty, though they might be rehabilitated through their own efforts or the intercession of others. Public attitudes shifted from an acknowledgment that the poor will always exist to the view that poverty was a social problem to be solved, and by government action rather than religious charity. Hence the growing popularity of poorhouses beginning in the 1820s. Outdoor relief, so the argument went, supported the slacker in his idleness, the drunkard in his inebriation, the gambler in his recklessness. Institutionalization, indoor relief, offered the chance of correction through discipline. The Staten Island Poor Farm stood out among others of its kind because it was directed at the able bodied and demanded work from those who lived there; the labor helped inmates earn their keep, estimated at $0.55 per day, but also could improve their moral fiber.

But if the Poor Farm removed the indigent from the sources of temptation, it became itself a temptation to its administrators. In the post-Civil War era, when "Boss" Tweed and his Ring were lining their pockets with the spoils of municipal graft in New York City, the Richmond County Board of Supervisors saw opportunities to enrich themselves in the provisioning of the farm. A controlling faction plunged their hands into the till, dispensed jobs to cronies, and demanded kickbacks. According to Ira K. Morris, who published his two-volume history of Staten Island in 1898, they ran up bills for fancy groceries that certainly never appeared on the paupers' dinner plates and, an indication of ineptness, left expensive machinery to rust. Contracts for manure "came up like annual reminders that somebody was lying in wait for a share in the appropriations." The poorhouse, concluded Morris, exuded "a stench in the nostrils of every decent citizen of the County." In 1890, after years of abuses, the corrupt officials were ousted from office, thanks in part to a campaign by the *Staten Island Standard*.

In 1898, the city assumed control and the Staten Island Poor Farm became, euphemistically, the New York City Farm Colony. Because the physical plant was dilapidated and the buildings poorly designed, the City undertook to expand the campus, constructing dormitories whose Dutch Colonial style evoked an early farming community. The Farm Colony deliberately avoided an institutional appearance and even built "cottages" so that elderly couples could live together instead of being segregated into same-sex dormitories. This, for its time, was an unusual gesture of humanity.

Although the Farm Colony had originally been intended to serve the able bodied, changes in citywide policies resulted in its gradually developing into a haven for the elderly. The enactment of the first federal Social Security legislation in 1935 spelled the beginning of the end for the Farm Colony. By 1950, when photographer Alice Austen (*see p. 126*) moved there, it had become bedraggled: the beds were iron, each illuminated by a naked light bulb dangling from the ceiling; the wards were noisy with the buzzing of flies and the babble of the patients, some of them demented. The social programs of the 1960s nudged the Farm Colony further down the road to oblivion, and the last residents moved out in 1975.

Declared part of the Farm Colony–Sea View Historic District in 1985, the Farm Colony is derelict today, its roofless buildings assaulted by the weather and encroaching vegetation. Although a chain link fence surrounds the property, it still attracts vandals, graffitists, paintballers, and the occasional photographer with an eye for ruins. The City of New York, the current owner, has put out requests for interest in redeveloping the site but so far there have been no takers.

SEAVIEW HOSPITAL: A MODEL SANITARIUM

At the dedication of Seaview Hospital in 1913, scientists, politicians, and philanthropists lauded it as both healthful and beautiful, worth every penny of the $4 million it had cost the City. In full triumphalist mode, they asserted that Seaview was the greatest TB hospital ever planned, the decade's most important event in the world-wide fight against the "white plague." No expense had been spared; the *New York Times* enthusiastically noted that the eaves of Seaview's buildings and even the top of the power-house chimney were inlaid with gold leaf—an exaggeration, since it was Delft tiles and not actual gold that glistened on high.

Seaview exemplified both New York City's pioneering struggle against tuberculosis and, once again, Staten Island's role in accepting society's unwanted.

The Sanitarium Movement

Before 1882, when Robert Koch isolated the tuberculosis bacillus, TB was usually considered hereditary because multiple cases often occurred in families. Nonetheless, it was also weighted with moral baggage. In an age when infection was poorly understood and hygiene standards were low, the medical profession struggled to make sense of things in ways that seem ludicrous in our days of over-the-counter antibiotics. Risk factors for TB were said to include pleasure-seeking, improper clothing of suspect bodily regions (for example, low necklines), and the catch-all vices of drink, sexual indulgence, and masturbation. Women who rode astride (as opposed to sidesaddle) might succumb to vice, which in turn could open the door to TB. Even celibacy was cited as a predisposing factor: a British physician noted in 1869 that in France's Catholic convents not more than one in ten entrants survived her novitiate before succumbing to the dread disease.

But though Koch discovered the cause of the disease, his discovery yielded no cure, and for the next eighty years its treatment remained at best common sense, and at worst, wild guesswork. "Cures" abounded: blood-letting, cupping, sea voyages, inhalations, cod liver oil, gold salts, patent medicines, even spiritual fulfillment. The core therapy, however, involved rest, nutritious food, fresh air, and plenty of sunlight. But Koch's isolation of the tuberculosis bacillus did at least cement recognition of TB as an infectious disease whose spread could be thwarted to some degree by public health measures. In 1889, with about 12,000 new cases occurring annually, New York became the first American city to declare tuberculosis a communicable disease. Two years later, the City required all public institutions to report cases of TB. It offered free diagnosis and undertook to segregate TB patients in separate wards. In 1904, as the number of cases tripled, the Department of Public Charities began thinking about establishing a TB hospital somewhere nearby.

Dr. Edward Livingston Trudeau, who had cared for a brother who died of TB and was diagnosed with it himself in 1873, fathered the sanitarium movement in the US. Emaciated and feverish, believing his days were numbered, he opted to live out his earthly existence in the Adirondack Mountains, at Saranac Lake, where he rested and went fishing. He gained fifteen pounds and returned to New York City, only to relapse. Eventually he relocated permanently to Saranac Lake, where in 1885 he established the Adirondack Cottage Community, the first American tuberculosis facility for people of moderate income.

Seaview as a model sanitarium

Seaview met all the criteria Trudeau had established for a tuberculosis facility. Sited on high ground, it offered serene vistas across gardens and woodlands to the sea. The altitude and the views were equally therapeutic, the former presumably offering "thinner" air that was easier to breathe, the latter helping patients avoid the depression that understandably accompanied long periods of confinement. Furthermore Seaview, while isolated from the rest of the City, was still accessible.

The buildings were designed for maximum air and light by Brooklyn-born, Paris-educated architect Raymond F. Almirall. His 1905 plans depict low buildings situated to receive maximum sunlight, smooth wall surfaces to prevent the accumulation of dust, large windows with cross-ventilation, and multi-storied open porches. Walking paths wound through lawns and woodlands with pagodas and gazebos placed here and there for resting.

A cure for TB: Seaview's success and demise

It was not until 1943 when Selman A. Waksman and his graduate student Albert Schatz discovered streptomycin that a non-toxic antibiotic was developed to arrest the growth of the tuberculosis bacillus. The new antibiotic revolutionized the treatment of TB and for the first time in centuries offered hope.

Streptomycin was not perfect. *M. tuberculosis* developed resistance to it; the drug was expensive and difficult to produce in quantity; it could affect hearing and the production of red blood cells. In 1951 at Seaview, Drs. Edward Robitzek and Irving Selikoff conducted the first clinical trials of another anti-tuberculosis drug, isoniazid, and reported that forty-four consecutive patients—all of them feverish, emaciated, and near death—showed rapid improvement. The announcement prompted a media circus. Reporters and news photographers descended on Seaview, snapping "before" and "after" photos—people formerly at death's door now dancing in the wards; the *New York Times* reported the story on page one. Isoniazid was cheap and easy to produce, reducing the cost of treatment per patient from $3,500 to $100, though it was most effective as part of a combination therapy.

Seaview's success brought its demise as a tuberculosis hospital. Patients recovered and were discharged, the last in 1961. Today, with tuberculosis more or less under control, some of Seaview's buildings stand empty; some have been leveled, and others have been repurposed. Over the years, new medical centers, services for the blind, a dental clinic, and a brain injury center were built here. Today the Staten Island Ballet occupies part of the former morgue, while other buildings have been restored as the Seaview Rehabilitation Center & Home (*map p. 261, D3*).

WILLOWBROOK

The name was bucolic—Willowbrook—taken from a stream that arose in the central Staten Island hills and meandered down through the western marshes into the Arthur Kill. Even in the days when Willowbrook State School was a horrific place, the setting still suggested a college campus, with some forty low-rise buildings on almost four hundred acres with green lawns and trees. The imposing hospital building even reminded one visitor of a cathedral.

But indoors, Willowbrook was Dantesque in its horror. Intended as a place where the severely mentally retarded could receive therapy and training, it had become instead a holding pen, a warehouse of misery where patients young and old were confined in locked wards and left more or less to rot. It was underfunded and understaffed, neglected by the state that had created it.

If an institution can be born under an evil star, then some malign force must have overseen the Willowbrook State School from its creation until its demise. In 1938, the State of New York drew up plans for an institution for the mentally retarded, but during World War II the place became a hospital for treating wounded veterans. The State of New York wrested Willowbrook back from the army in 1947 and the first patients began coming in the 1950s. By the end of that decade, Willowbrook was crowded with disabled people whose families could not or would not care for them and whom other institutions fobbed off. Once again Staten Island was the end of the road, on the receiving end of what the rest of the City or State did not want to look at or think about.

In 1965, Robert Kennedy, then senator for New York State, showed up unannounced. Appalled at what he saw—"snake pit," "filth and dirt," "less comfortable than the cages...at the zoo"—he testified before the state commission on mental retardation. But when the spotlight followed him to Washington, the Willowbrook State School lapsed into its accustomed ways.

On 4 January 1972, Michael Wilkins, a young doctor without civil service tenure, received a pink slip telling him to clear out his belongings and leave. He knew why. He and his colleague Dr. William Bronston had agitated to improve conditions at the school, demanding larger appropriations, even approaching the press. Both men had come to Staten Island after working in the city's most troubled neighborhoods; both men were activists.

And the supervisor who fired Wilkins made a crucial mistake. He did not confiscate Wilkins's key.

Wilkins approached Geraldo Rivera, at the time a rookie television news reporter. Rivera arrived with a film crew the next day. Wilkins unlocked the outer doors to Building 6 and then the heavy metal inner doors. Rivera and his crew were shocked at what they saw, as were the viewers who watched the film on that evening's news.

Emboldened by the exposure on TV, parents' groups

aided by civil rights lawyers filed a class-action suit in federal court against the State of New York, litigating to have Willowbrook closed and its residents transferred to group homes in the community. The case dragged on, but in 1975, the Willowbrook Consent Decree mandated increased community placement and improvements to the school. The decree formally recognized that "retarded persons regardless of the degree of handicapping conditions are capable of physical, intellectual, psychological and social growth." It mandated standards of care that included guidelines on staffing, diet, education, cleanliness, physical therapy, psychological services, and so on. The legal and organizational challenges proved daunting, and only in 1987, twelve years after the decree was signed, did the last patients move out of Willowbrook. After forty harrowing years, Willowbrook State School finally closed. The Willowbrook "wars" had a profound impact on the treatment and the civil rights of the developmentally disabled in New York State and the rest of the nation.

In September 1987, the state transferred ownership of Willowbrook to the College of Staten Island, part of the City University of New York, whose facilities had been scattered around the borough. The college renovated some of the buildings and tore down or abandoned others. With the opening of the campus for the College in 1993, Willowbrook (*map p. 260, C3*) became what it was intended to be—a school.

PRACTICAL INFORMATION

When you visit (contact listings)—Transportation—Hotels—
Staten Island restaurants

WHEN YOU VISIT

An alphabetical list of the Staten Island sights described in
this book, with full contact information.

Alice Austen House

Spectacular view of the
Narrows and the Verrazano-
Narrows Bridge. Historic
house exhales a sense of a
gentler, kinder past. Exhib-
its of Austen photographs.
Contact: *2 Hylan Blvd. T:*
718.816.4506; aliceausten.
org. Map p. 261, F2.
Transportation: *A 15-minute*
ride on bus S51 from the
St. George Ferry Terminal
to Hylan Blvd and Bay St.
Walk one block toward the
water on Hylan Blvd.
Open: *Tues–Sun 11–5; closed*
Jan and Feb, major holidays.
Grounds open every day
until dusk.
Restaurants: *On nearby*
Bay St: Montalbano, Ital-
ian Deli, 1140 Bay St, T:
718.448.8077; Tony's Brick
Oven Pizza, 1140 Bay St,
T: 718.816.6516; Bay Street
Luncheonette, 1189 Bay St,
T: 718.720.0922.
In the neighborhood:
Garibaldi-Meucci House,
Fort Wadsworth.

Conference House

Historic house with period

furniture and cellar kitchen, exhibits, events. Beautiful water views, even with New Jersey's industrial shoreline in the background; walking trails including one to the southernmost point in New York State, locally known as "the South Pole," a literal red post stuck into the ground.

Contact: *Visitors Center, 298 Satterlee St. T: 718.984.6046; www.conferencehouse.org. Map p. 262, A7.*

Open: *Tours are given Fri–Sun 1–4 from first weekend in April until mid-Dec.*

Transportation: *Bus S59 (Richmond Ave) or S78 Tottenville (Hylan Blvd) to Hylan Blvd and Craig Ave. Walk one block south to Conference House Park. Or Staten Island Railway to the last stop, Tottenville. Exit near intersection of Main St and Utah St. Walk south on Main St. Turn right onto Craig Ave. Turn right onto Hylan Blvd. Turn left onto Satterlee St for the Visitors Center or right towards the Conference House. Walk takes about 15mins.*

Restaurants: *Towne Deli, 5373 Arthur Kill Rd, T: 718.227.1985; Angelina's, 399 Ellis St, T: 718.227.2900; Dock's Clam Bar, 240 Page Ave, T: 718.227.8500; Egger's Ice Cream Parlor, 7437 Amboy Rd, T: 718.605.9335.*

Fort Wadsworth

Historic fort, spectacular views of the harbor and the Verrazano-Narrows Bridge. Walking trails. Seasonal visitor center at the entrance with maps, information.

Access: *210 New York Ave (the extension of Bay St). T: 718.354.4500 (Gateway*

National Recreation Area); www.nps.gov/gate. Map p. 261, F2–F3.

Open: Overlook open dawn to dusk. No food service at the park.

Transportation: Bus S51 from the Ferry Terminal. Weekdays the bus stops inside the Fort; weekends the bus stops just outside of Fort Wadsworth at Von Briesen Park and you must walk into the Fort.

Restaurants: Basilio Inn, 6 Galesville Court, T: 718.447.9292; Italianissimo, 107 McClean Ave, T: 718.442.4442.

In the neighborhood: Miller Field, Great Kills Park, Alice Austen House, Garibaldi-Meucci Museum.

Frederick Law Olmsted on Staten Island

Unfortunately Olmsted left few footprints on Staten Island (you can visit his masterpieces in Manhattan and Brooklyn). The **Olmsted-Beil House** at 4515 Hylan Blvd (up a long driveway and not visible from the main road; *map p. 263, D5*) is owned by the New York City Department of Parks and Recreation and is only open to the public for special events. Olmsted lived in the house in 1848–50 and again in 1858 when he was designing Central Park, moving to Manhattan in 1859; the property remained in his family until 1866. The house was owned for forty years by the family of Staten Island naturalist Carlton B. Beil, who sold it to the Parks Department.

The **Vanderbilt Mausoleum** in the Moravian Cemetery (*map p. 261, D3*), for which Olmsted designed the landscaping, is not open to the public.

The Greenbelt

The Greenbelt Conservancy has downloadable hiking maps at www.sigreenbelt. org. Also available at the Greenbelt Nature Center, T: 718.667.2165. Most of the Greenbelt sites are mid-Island and involve fairly long bus rides.

Freshkills Park: A new park in the making; 2,200 acres of formerly abused land being reclaimed over the next thirty years as a park. As of early 2013, only the Schmul Playground and some soccer fields are open regularly. Sneak Peeks are held annually for the public; you may also book a tour. Check the NYC Parks Department–Freshkills web site: *www.nycgovparks.org/ park-features/freshkills-park/ tours-and-events#public_ tours.*

Greenbelt Nature Center: The Greenbelt Nature Center opened in 2004, with state-of-the-art exhibits. Guided nature hikes, lectures, environmental education, even yoga classes.
Contact: 700 Rockland Ave (at Brielle Ave). T: 718.351.3450. Map p. 261, D3.
Open: April–Oct, Tues–Sun 10–5. Nov–March, Wed–Sun 11–5.
Transportation: From the Ferry Terminal, S62 bus to Bradley Ave. Transfer to the S57 bus, to the Brielle and Rockland Ave stop. Cross the street at the light.

High Rock Park: A 90.5-acre nature preserve with

hiking trails, guided hikes, nature education, picnic grounds, restrooms.

Contact: *200 Nevada Ave. T: 718.667.2165; www.sigreenbelt.org. Map p. 261, D3.*

Transportation: *Bus S74 from the St. George Ferry Terminal to Rose Ave; S57 to Rockland Ave; walk up Nevada Ave through the parking lot and up the hill to the park.*

Moravian Cemetery: One hundred thirteen acres on the eastern edge of High Rock Park, landscaped with lakes, trees, flowering shrubs, and plantings; more than 80 miles of paths and roads; guided tours, genealogy assistance.

Contact: *2205 Richmond Rd. T: 718.351.0136; www.moraviancemetery.com. Map p. 261, D3. For seasonal tours (Sun at 2pm), contact* *historian Richard L. Simpson at cemeteryguy@earthlink.net.*

Open: *Gates open daily 8–6:30 (close later during summer), weather permitting.*

Transportation: *Staten Island Railroad from Ferry Terminal to Grant City stop; walk two blocks along Fremont Ave to Richmond Rd. Left on Richmond Rd, right on Todt Hill Rd; walk up the hill to cemetery entrance. Or bus S74, S76 to corner of Richmond Rd and Todt Hill Rd; short walk up the hill to the church. There is also a gate on Richmond Rd, opposite Otis St.*

Moses' Mountain: A c. 200-foot "mountain" offering a panoramic view, formed when boulders and serpentine rock were dug up to build Robert Moses' unfinished Richmond Parkway in the 1960s.

Access: Map p. 261, D3. Accessible from the Yellow Trail in the Greenbelt System.

Transportation: From the Ferry Terminal, S62 bus to Bradley Ave. Transfer to the S57 bus, to intersection of Rockland Ave and Manor Rd. The trailhead (Yellow Trail) is off the north side (Manor Rd side) of Rockland Ave about 30 yards from the intersection, behind a metal barrier.

William T. Davis Wildlife Refuge: The Refuge, adjoining Freshkills Park, has an easy half-mile hiking trail, the Pink Trail of the Greenbelt trail system; it passes through wetlands, fields and forest, offering excellent bird watching.

Access: Located at the northern edge of Freshkills Park, south of Signs Rd and east of Victory Blvd. Entrance off Travis Ave near Mulberry Ave; limited parking on neighborhood streets. Map p. 260, D3.

Transportation: From St. George Ferry Terminal, bus S92 via Victory Blvd to Richmond Ave; Richmond Ave to Travis Ave. Walk about 0.3 miles to park.

Historic Richmond Town

Outdoor history museum on the site of Staten Island's early government center. Guided tours, historic buildings, demonstrations, special events.

Historical Museum: The star attractions in the permanent exhibit of Americana and Staten-Islandiana are a Staten Island skiff and historic oystering tools: tongs (long, heavy, unwieldy), rakes, scoops and baskets, and a foot-long oyster shell. Also, an exhibit on the Verrazano-Narrows Bridge with architectural drawings and plans, and a street marker from 1984 with wooden flags pointing to new developments in every which direction.

Access: *441 Clarke Ave (bounded by Richmond Rd, and Arthur Kill Rd). Parking lot off Clarke Ave. T: 718.351.1611. www. historicrichmondtown.org. Map p. 261, D4.*

Open: *Wed–Sun 1–5. Closed major holidays.*

Transportation: *Bus S74 from the St. George Ferry Terminal to Richmond Rd and St. Patrick's Pl, half an hour or more depending on traffic.*

Restaurant: *Bennett Café, run by volunteers, open for lunch Thur–Sat (espe-cially in peak season); call to confirm, T: 718.351.1611, x256.*

In the neighborhood: *Jacques Marchais Museum of Tibetan Art; Lighthouse Hill with Staten Island Range Light and Frank Lloyd Wright's "Crimson Beech"; St. Andrew's Church and Cemetery.*

Italian Staten Island

Garibaldi-Meucci Museum:
Victorian Gothic cottage; exhibits include one of Garibaldi's red shirts, a model of Meucci's telephone, and artifacts recreating the ambiance of the era. In the back yard stands a huge kettle where the two men melted tallow for candles.

Access: *420 Tompkins Ave; entrance on Chestnut Ave. T: 718.442.1608; www.*

garibaldimeuccimuseum.org.
Map p. 261, F2.

Open: *Wed–Sat 1–5; last tour
at 4:30. Closed Sun, Mon,
and Tues.*

Transportation: *Bus S78 or
S52 from the Ferry to Tompkins and Chestnut Aves.*

In the neighborhood:
*Alice Austen House, Fort
Wadsworth, Shrine of Our
Lady of Mount Carmel.*

Pizza and gelato: There
are plenty of places to buy
pizza and Italian ice on
Staten Island, but two have
achieved legendary status.
**Denino's Pizzeria and Tav-
ern**; a historic family business that opened in 1937.
Carlo Denino, son of the
founders, is credited with
adding pizza to the menu
(*524 Port Richmond Ave, T:
718.442.9401. Map p. 260,
C2*); and **Ralph's Famous
Italian Ices** (*501 Port Richmond Ave, T: 718.273.3675*).
After selling ices from a
truck since 1928, Ralph
Silvestro opened his store
in Port Richmond in 1945.
Ralph's has become a fran-
chise (*see www.ralphsices.com
for other locations*).

**Shrine of Our Lady of
Mount Carmel:** Folk-art
shrine tucked away on a
quiet side street.

Access: *36 Amity St, off
White Plains Ave. You may
need a detailed map to find
this secluded place. Map p.
261, F2.*

Transportation: *Bus S78
or S52 from the Ferry to
Tompkins and St. Mary's
Aves. Walk down St. Mary's
Ave away from the water
(against the one-way traffic); left on White Plains
Ave, right on Amity St. The
shrine is half way down the
block on the left.*

Restaurants: Same as Alice Austen House; see p. 209.

In the neighborhood: Alice Austen House, Garibaldi-Meucci Museum, Fort Wadsworth.

Lighthouse Hill

The Jacques Marchais Museum of Tibetan Art:

Tibetan art in a serene hillside setting designed to resemble a Himalayan monastery.

Access: 338 Lighthouse Ave. T: 718.987.3500; www. tibetanmuseum.org. Map p. 261, D4.

Open: April–Nov, Wed–Sun, 1pm–5pm; Dec–March, Fri–Sun 1pm—5pm. Check web site for holiday closings.

Transportation: S74 bus from the St. George Ferry Terminal to Lighthouse Ave; walk up the hill, slightly less than a half mile. Taxi service from the Staten Island Ferry.

Restaurants: No food service at the museum or nearby.

In the neighborhood: The Staten Island Range Light, best seen from Edinboro Rd; Frank Lloyd Wright's only New York house, "Crimson Beech," at 48 Manor Court; Historic Richmond Town.

Snug Harbor Cultural Center and Botanical Garden

The Greek Revival and other historic buildings of Sailors' Snug Harbor have been repurposed to accommodate exhibition and performance spaces, artists' studios, and educational facilities. Also on the grounds are a statue of *Neptune* (replica outdoors, the real thing indoors), the monument to Robert Richard Randall (also a replica), the Chapel, the former Music Hall, the

Staten Island Children's Museum.

Access: 1000 Richmond Terrace. T: 718.448.2500; www.snug-harbor.org. Map p. 261, E1.

Open: Grounds open daily, dawn to dusk. Chinese Scholar's Garden open Tues–Sun 10am–4pm. Visitors' Center and Art Galleries open Wed–Sun noon to 5pm. Noble Maritime Collection open Thur–Sun 1pm–5pm.

Transportation: S40 bus from the St. George Ferry Terminal to Snug Harbor.

Restaurants: Garden Grill located next to the green house and an outdoor lunch-eonette are open May–Sept noon to 4pm. Picnicking on the Snug Harbor grounds. Restaurants in the neighbor-hood include Adobe Blues, 63 Lafayette Ave near Fill-more Ave, exit from the east gate, T: 718.720.2583; Blue, 1115 Richmond Terrace, exit through the west gate, T: 718.273.7777; Crispy Pizza, 782 Richmond Ter-race, corner of Clinton Ave, T: 718.420.6050.

Newhouse Center for Contemporary Art: The Newhouse Center was founded in 1977 with a focus on Staten Island artists or on those whose work reflects the history of Staten Island or Snug Harbor, though today its focus has widened to embrace contemporary art in general. The gallery is unusual in its expansive exhibition space and grounds which can encompass outdoor exhibits. *Building G. Open Wed–Sun noon–5pm. T: 718.448.2500.*

Staten Island Botanical Garden: Founded in 1977, the Staten Island Botanical Garden now encompasses 53 acres and includes 20 specimen gardens. Among them are a Tuscan garden designed after the Villa Gamberaia in Florence, a White Garden inspired by Vita Sackville-West's garden at Sissinghurst, and a Garden of Healing with the World Trade Center Educational Tribute. The walled Chinese Scholar's Garden, a series of open-air courtyards, pavilions, and ponds is modeled after a fifteenth-century Ming Dynasty garden and is planted with roses, chrysanthemums, and magnolias. *Grounds open daily dawn to dusk. Chinese Scholar's Garden open Tues–Sun 10am–4pm. T: 718.425.3504.*

On the grounds of Snug Harbor Cultural Center

Noble Maritime Collection: Museum in a beautifully restored sailors' dormitory showcasing John A. Noble's paintings, drawings, and prints; his floating studio as well as a reconstruction of his father's atelier in Picardy; and exhibits of contemporary and historical art. *Building D. Open Thur–Sun 1–5pm. T: 718.447.6490; www. noblemaritime.org.*

Staten Island Museum: *NB: The Staten Island Museum History Center and Historical Archives are located at the Snug Harbor Cultural Center, 1000 Richmond Terrace, Building H, T: 718. 727.1135, x122; call for hours. At the time of writing, the museum was scheduled to* move its exhibition space to Building A at Snug Harbor. A fine small museum, whose natural history collection—shells, stuffed birds and animals, plants, minerals, and especially insects (cicadas, beetles, butterflies)—reflects the interests of the Island's passionate collectors and naturalists. Art and history collections (including por-traits of the aforementioned collectors and scientists). Permanent exhibitions on Lenape Indians, the Ferry. *Access* (*until the museum moves to Snug Harbor*): 75 Stuyvesant Pl (Wall St).

T: 718.727.1135; www. statenislandmuseum.org.
Open: Mon–Fri 11–5; Sat 10–5; Sun noon–5. Closed New Year's Day, Memorial Day, Independence Day, Labor Day, Thanksgiving, and Christmas Day.
Restaurants: No café, but restaurants nearby: Ruddy & Dean, 44 Richmond Terrace, T: 718.816.4400; Beso, 11 Schuyler St, T: 718.816.8162; A&S Piz-zeria, 87 Stuyvesant Pl, T: 718.448.4142.
In the neighborhood: Staten Island Ferry, Staten Island 9/11 Memorial.

TRANSPORTATION

Getting to Staten Island

Unless you have a car, you will get to Staten Island on the Ferry, which leaves from the Staten Island Ferry Whitehall Terminal at the southern tip of Manhattan. The nearest sub-way stops in Manhattan are the J/Z to Broad Street, 4/5 to

Bowling Green, R to Whitehall St, or 1 to South Ferry (*NB: As of February 2013 there was no service until further notice on the 1 train between Rector St and South Ferry. If this is the case, use the 4/5 to Bowling Green or the R to Whitehall St instead*).

The Ferry is free and runs seven days a week, 24 hours a day; boats are frequent during rush hours, half-hourly during most other times, and longer between midnight and 6am. Holiday service operates every half hour from 7am–11pm on New Years Day, Presidents' Day, Memorial Day, July 4, Labor Day, Thanksgiving and Christmas; after 11pm, hourly service. Schedule may change in case of heavy weather or reduced visibility. Check www.nyc.gov/dot or call 311.

Getting around the Island

Several points of interest are located in St. George near the Ferry Terminal, accessible on foot or by a short bus ride. Many bus lines depart from the terminal, but it's easier to visit more distant sites by car. The Staten Island Railroad (SIR) runs from St. George south to Tottenville. The line and all stations are marked on the maps at the back of this book.

Web sites and apps

The New York City official tourist bureau's web site for Staten Island, www.visitstatenisland.com, has practical information on car rentals, car services, public transportation, and other tourist services, as well as maps.

Numerous apps for mobile phones tackle the NYC transit system: visit mta.info/apps.

HOTELS

Hotels from the major chains are located near the expressways and are convenient if you have a car. Otherwise you might prefer day trips from Manhattan.

Hampton Inn and Suites. *1120 South Ave; off the West Shore Expressway in Graniteville. Map p. 260, B3. T: 718.477.1600; hamptoninn3.hilton.com.*

Holiday Inn Express–Staten Island West. *300 Wild Ave; off the West Shore Expressway, Victory Blvd exit. Map p. 260, B4. T: 718.370.8777; www.holidayinn.com.*

Hilton Garden Inn New York/Staten Island. *1100 South Ave; off the West Shore Expressway, in Graniteville. Map p. 262, B2. T: 718.477.2400; hiltongardeninn3.hilton.com.*

STATEN ISLAND RESTAURANTS

Places to eat, culled from the recommendations of Staten Islanders, reviews, and personal experience.

Adobe Blues. *63 Lafayette Ave (Fillmore St), West Brighton. T: 718.720.2583. Map p. 261, E1.* Cantina-style Tex-Mex, many beer choices, reputedly good food.

Andrew's Diner. *4160 Hylan Blvd (Walnut Ave), Great Kills. T: 718.948.8544; AndrewsDiner.com. Map p. 263, D5.*
Classic diner menu, Greek and Italian specialties.

Angelina's Ristorante. *399 Ellis St (off Arthur Kill Rd), Tottenville, near the railroad station. T: 718.227.2900; angelinasristorante.com. Map p. 262, A7.*
Italian food, on the water at the Island's southern tip. Closed Mon.

Bayou. *1072 Bay St (Chestnut St), Clifton-Rosebank. T: 718.273.4383; www.bayounyc.com. Map p. 261, F2.*
Cajun-Creole.

Beso. *11 Schuyler St (Richmond Terrace), St. George. T: 718.816 8162; besonyc.com. Map p. 261, E1.*
A short walk from the Ferry. Spanish, tapas.

Blue. *1115 Richmond Terrace (Kissel Ave), Randall Manor. T: 718.273.7777; bluerestaurantnyc.com. Map p. 261, D1.*
Uses produce from Snug Harbor Heritage Farm.

Brioso. *174 New Dorp Lane (9th St), New Dorp. T: 718.667.1700; briosoristorante.com. Map p. 261, E4.*
Italian-Mediterranean, family restaurant.

Brother's Pizza. *750 Port Richmond Ave (Willowbrook Rd), Elm Park. T: 718.442.2332. Map p. 260, C2.*
Old-fashioned pizza place.

Carol's Café. *1571 Richmond Rd (Flagg Place), Todt Hill. T: 718.979.5600; carolscafe.com. Map p. 261, E3.*

Eclectic menu, cozy atmosphere.

Da Noi. *4358 Victory Blvd (Crabbs Lane), Travis. T: 718.982.5040; danoirestaurant.com. Map p. 260, B4. Also at 138 Fingerboard Rd (Tompkins Ave), Shore Acres. T: 718.720.1650; danoirestaurant.com. Map p. 261, F2.* Neighborhood Italian.

Denino's. *524 Port Richmond Ave (Hooker Place), Port Richmond. T: 718.442.9401; deninos.com. Map p. 260, C2.* Famous pizza, casual dining.

Dosa Garden. *323 Victory Blvd (Cebra Ave), Tompkinsville. T: 718.420.0919; dosagardenny.com. Map p. 261, E1.* In Little Sri Lanka; South Indian, many vegetarian dishes. No lunch Mon.

Enoteca Maria. *27 Hyatt St (Central Ave), St. George. T: 718.447.2777; enotecamaria. com. Map p. 261, E1.* Italian grandmas in the kitchen; intimate; good wine list; no credit cards. Closed Mon, Tues. Dinner only.

Joe & Pat's. *1758 Victory Blvd (Manor Rd), Castleton Corners. T: 718.981.0887; joeandpatspizzany.com. Map p. 261, D2.* Classic pizzeria, seafood, family restaurant.

Lakruwana. *668 Bay St (Broad St), Stapleton. T: 347.857.6619; lakruwana. com. Map p. 261, E2–F2.* Good Sri Lankan.

Pasticceria Bruno. *676 Forest Ave (Bement Ave), West Brighton. T: 718.448.0993; pasticceriabruno.com. Map p.*

261, D2.
Popular restaurant and bakery. Open for breakfast lunch and dinner, seven days a week.

Rick's Café. *695 Bay St (Broad St), Stapleton. T: 718.727.FOOD (3663); rickscafesi.com. Map p. 261, E2–F2.*
Café and wine bar; good views. Closed Sun, Mon.

South Fin Grill. *300 Father Capodanno Blvd (Sand Lane), Arrochar. T: 718.447.7679; southfingrill.com. Map p. 261, F3.*
Seafood on the Boardwalk; restricted hours in winter.

Trattoria Romana.
1476 Hylan Blvd (Benton Ave), South Beach. T: 718.980.3113. Map p. 261, E3.

Popular Italian, casual, neighborhood favorite.

Vida. *381 Van Duzer St (Beach St), Stapleton. T: 718.720.1501; vidany.com. Map p. 261, E1–E2.*
Small, eclectic. Closed Sun, Mon. No lunch Tues, Wed, Thur.

Zest. *977 Bay St (Willow Ave), Rosebank. T: 718.390.8477; zestaurant. com. Map p. 261, F2.*
French-American bistro; outdoor garden. Closed Mon. Dinner only.

FURTHER READING

Abbott, Mabel and Edwin Way Teale. *The Life of William T. Davis*. Ithaca, NY: Cornell University Press, 1949. A delightful recounting of the naturalist's life. Available as a photographic reprint.

Ballon, Hilary, and Kenneth T. Jackson, eds. *Robert Moses and the Modern City: The Transformation of New York*. New York: W.W. Norton & Company, 2007. Reappraisal of Moses' impact on New York.

Caro, Robert A. *The Power Broker: Robert Moses and the Fall of New York*. New York: Knopf, 1974. Classic Pulitzer-Prize-winning biography of a complex man.

Davis, William T. *Days Afield on Staten Island*. Staten Island, NY: Staten Island Institute of Arts and Sciences, 1892. Commemorative ed., 1992. Davis's delightful and nostalgic recollections of his "tramps" on an unspoiled Staten Island.

Fein, Albert. *Landscape into Cityscape: Frederick Law Olmsted's Plans for a Greater New York City*. Ithaca, NY: Cornell University Press, 1968. Includes the Commissioners' Report of 1871, with Frederick Law Olmsted's recommendations for a chain of parks.

Gold, Kenneth M., and Lori R. Weintrob, eds. *Discovering Staten Island: A 350th Anniversary Commemorative History*. Charleston, SC: The History Press, 2011. A useful compendium of information about Staten Island today: history, social life, arts, sports, food and drink, etc. Written by knowledgeable Staten Islanders.

Jackson, Kenneth T., ed. *The Encyclopedia of New York City*. 2nd ed. New Haven: Yale University Press, and New York: The New-York Historical Society, 2010. The best all-around source of information about New York.

Kurlansky, Mark. *The Big Oyster: History on the Half Shell*. New York: Ballantine Books, 2006. Entertaining account of oysters, their biology, ecology, and history.

Leng, Charles W. and William T. Davis. *Staten Island and Its People, a History, 1609–1929*. 5 vols. New York: Lewis Historical Publishing Company, 1929–1933. The most detailed and comprehensive history of Staten Island ever published, unfortunately out of print and difficult to obtain. The first two volumes are historical, the last three biographical.

Matteo, Thomas W. *Staten Island Then & Now*. Charleston, SC: Arcadia Publishing, 2006. Illuminating "before and after" photos gleaned from the collections of the Staten Island Institute of Arts & Sciences accompanied by informative text. Dr. Matteo is the present Staten Island borough historian.

———— *Staten Island: I Didn't Know That*. Virginia Beach, VA: Donning Company, 2010. A compendium of interesting, sometimes oddball, facts about Staten Island organized by topic; excellent photos, index and bibliography.

Miller, Benjamin. *Fat of the Land: Garbage in New York, The Last Two Hundred Years*. New York: Four Walls Eight Windows, 2000. All the dirt about New York's garbage, including the politics.

Mitchell, John G. *High Rock and the Greenbelt: The Making of New York City's Largest Park*. Edited by Charles E. Little. The Center for American Places at Columbia College Chicago, 2011. Rev. ed. of *High Rock*. New York: Friends of High Rock, 1976. A full account of the struggle to create and preserve the Greenbelt.

Mosley, Lois A. *Sandy Ground Memories*. Introduction and additional essays by Barnett Shepherd. Staten Island, NY: The Staten Island Historical Society, 2003. Recollections of life in Sandy Ground, with photos of historic buildings and reminiscences of other residents.

Novotny, Ann. *Alice's World: The Life and Photography of an American Original*. Chatham Press, 1976. The definitive work on Alice Austen.

Papas, Philip. *That Ever Loyal Island: Staten Island and the American Revolution*. New York, New York University Press, 2007. Scholarly book on Staten Island during the Revolution.

Rastdorfer, Darl. *Six Bridges: The Legacy of Othmar H. Ammann*. New Haven and London: Yale University Press, 2000. Beautiful photos and a thorough discussion of Ammann's life and work.

Sachs, Charles L. *Made On Staten Island: Agriculture, Industry, and Suburban Living in the City*. Staten Island, NY: Staten Island Historical Society, 1988. Brief essays on the Island's principal industries. Some of the objects in the photos are on display in the Historical Society's permanent collection.

Salmon, Patricia M. *Realms of History: The Cemeteries of Staten Island. Staten Island, NY: Staten Island Institute of Arts & Sciences, 2006.

———— *The Staten Island Ferry: A History*. Staten Island, NY: Staten Island Museum, 2006. Ms. Salmon, Curator of History of the Staten Island Museum, has written two finely detailed books, both based on extensive documentary research and accompanied by illustrations.

Shepherd, Barnett. *Tottenville: The Town the Oyster Built: A Staten Island Community, Its People, Industry and Architecture*. Staten Island, NY: Preservation League of Staten Island: Tottenville Historical Society, 2008.

———— *Sailors' Snug Harbor: 1801–1976*. Staten Island, NY: Snug Harbor Cultural Center, 1979. Two excellent examples of local history by an independent historian and Staten Island preservationist.

Staten Island N.Y. Historic Book Collection. CD ROM. Anderson, SC: THA New Media LLC, 2009. Digital images of several early histories of Staten Island: Richard M. Bayles's *History of Richmond County, Staten Island, New York: From Its Discovery to the Present Time* (1887); John J. Clute's *Annals of Staten Island: From Its Discovery to the Present Time* (1877); and Ira K. Morris's *Memorial History of Staten Island, New York* (1898–1900).

Steinmeyer, Henry George. *Staten Island, 1524–1898*. Staten Island, NY: Staten Island Historical Society, 1961, rev. 1987. An entertaining short history of Staten Island.

Stiles, T.J. *The First Tycoon: The Epic Life of Cornelius Vanderbilt*. New York: Alfred A. Knopf, 2009. Engaging Pulitzer-

Prize-winning biography, with informative sections on Dutch Staten Island.

Talese, Gay. *The Bridge*. New York: Harper & Row, 1964. The building of the Verrazano-Narrows Bridge, its social consequences, and, especially, the story of the men who built it.

Urban, Erin. *Hulls and Hulks in the Tide of Time: The Life and Work of John A. Noble*. Staten Island, NY: John Noble and Allan A. Noble in association with the John A. Noble Collection Publishers, 1993. A beautifully written and beautifully illustrated book about a Staten Island artist who devoted his life to recording the passing of the age of sail.

———— *Caddell Dry Dock: 100 Years Harborside*. Staten Island, NY: The Noble Maritime Collection, 2009. The history of New York harbor's oldest operating shipyard, illustrated with historical and contemporary photos (the latter by Michael Falco, whose mural *Marsh Meets the Sea* hangs in the St. George Ferry Terminal).

Images

Arcadia Publishing's *Images of America*. Series offering pictorial books on local history, with text but no indexes. Photos range from personal snapshots to historical views; texts vary in quality. There are volumes devoted to individual neighborhoods, as well as to the Island's different ethnic communities.

Web site

Staten Island Advance: www. silive.com. Day-by-day happenings on Staten Island; historical feature stories.

STATEN ISLAND TIMELINE

1500:   An estimated 15,000 Lenape Indians live in the greater New York area. They hunt, gather, and eventually sow and reap, leaving shell middens along Staten Island's shore and establishing burial grounds at Ward's Point and elsewhere.

1524:   Giovanni da Verrazano, looking for a water route to the Far East, sails into the Narrows, where 400 years later Italian American New Yorkers will have a bridge named after him; his ship is driven out to sea and he leaves without going ashore.

1528:   Giovanni da Verrazano, on his third voyage to North America, is killed and eaten by cannibals, probably on Guadaloupe.

1609:   Henry Hudson sails into New York Bay and gives "Staaten Eylandt" its name to honor his employer, the States General of the Dutch government. The Lenapes greet him, but when some of the sailors go ashore, shoot and kill one of them. The Europeans retaliate.

1611:   Henry Hudson is marooned in a small open boat in Hudson Bay by mutinous sailors and is never seen again.

1614:   The Dutch are establishing fur-trading posts in New Netherland.

1624:   Nicolaes van Wassenaer, a physician and scholar, reports that excessive drinking has undermined the authority of at least one sachem. Cornelis May brings 30 families to New Netherland, mostly Walloons. They settle in the Hudson Valley and on Manhattan and Noten (now Governors) Island.

1625:   Dutch and Walloon settlers build Fort Amsterdam at the southern tip of Manhattan.

1628:   To encourage colonization, the Dutch West India Company offers large land grants (patroonships) to wealthy men provided they establish settlements of fifty people.

1630:   Michael Pauw is granted Staten Island and large tracts of New Jersey as his patroonship but his endeavor does not thrive and he sells back his rights to the Company seven years later.

1636:   David de Vries, a Dutch explorer and sea captain, is granted Staten Island.

1638:   Willem Kieft, a merchant with powerful family connections but a shady past, arrives as director of New Netherland. His policies toward the Indians will be catastrophic.

1639:   De Vries establishes a plantation on Staten Island. Kieft demands "tribute" from the Lenapes, which leads to friction. The Indians kill Dutch livestock, which has been trampling their crops.

1641:   The Pig War: the Indians allegedly kill some hogs belonging to David de Vries. The Dutch retaliate by killing three or four Indians and torturing the sachem's brother. The Indians retaliate by killing four farmers and burning De Vries's buildings.

1642: Another Dutch colonist is killed by an Indian in what is now Bayonne, New Jersey. Kieft vows to "wipe the mouths of the savages."

1643: Kieft's soldiers massacre 120 Lenapes as well as Indians from other groups in vicious surprise attacks in New Jersey and on Manhattan. The brutality, according to David de Vries would "move a heart of stone." The carnage provokes full-scale war as the Indians retaliate in what is called the Whiskey War. Staten Island settlements are abandoned.

1644: War continues, with the Dutch attacking Indian villages on Staten Island and elsewhere in New Netherland. Kieft loses support. New Amsterdam settlers blame Kieft's Indian policy for local devastation.

1645: War ends. Some 1,600 Indians and many colonists have died. Dozens of settlements are abandoned. Kieft is recalled to Holland.

1647: Peter Stuyvesant arrives to replace Kieft. His policies stabilize a precarious New Amsterdam.

1650: Cornelis Melyn, a merchant and director of the West India Company, arrives from Holland with a band of farmers and settles on Staten Island.

1655: The Peach War: an Indian woman is shot for picking a peach from a Dutch orchard on Manhattan. The Indians retaliate, killing settlers and burning farms. The Staten Island settlement is again abandoned.

1660:   Charles II, restored as King of England, grants Staten Island and other territory to his brother James, Duke of York.

1661–62: The first successful agricultural settlement, Oude Dorp (near present South Beach), is established by Dutch and French-speaking Protestants with the blessing of Peter Stuyvesant.

1663:   The Rev. Samuel Drisius comes twice a month to New Dorp to minister to the congregants.

1664:   Four English warships anchor in Gravesend Bay off Brooklyn. The English offer the Dutch in New Amsterdam generous terms of surrender. The Dutch, lacking food, weapons, and leadership, see no point in fighting the English on behalf of the Dutch West India Company. New Amsterdam becomes New York.

1670:   English governor Richard Lovelace "buys" Staten Island from the Lenape, whose concept of ownership differs fundamentally from European notions: they sell the "use of the land" but not the land itself, which in their eyes cannot "belong" to anyone.

1680:   New York governor Sir Edmund Andros dictates that all Indians are free people, not slaves.

1683:   Staten Island becomes Richmond County, named after the Duke of Richmond, illegitimate son of Charles II. Thomas Dongan is appointed governor of English New York. Petrus Tesschenmaker arrives on Staten Island to head the Dutch church.

1692: Huguenots settle on Staten Island.

1695: The Voorlezer's house is built at Richmondtown, then called Cocclestown; it is today the oldest schoolhouse in the US.

1700: In the early 18th century ferries begin running from the North Shore to Manhattan and also across the Narrows to Brooklyn.

1705: Richmond Terrace is being laid out.

1715: Dutch families are concentrated on the North Shore near Port Richmond; they build the Reformed Dutch Church, on the site of the present Staten Island Reformed Church.

1776: On July 2–3, a British fleet anchors in the Lower Bay. Nine thousand troops come ashore to be welcomed wholeheartedly by most Staten Islanders, many of whom declare allegiance to the king. July 9, Staten Islanders hear of the signing of the Declaration of Independence. September 11, peace conference held at home of Christopher Billopp, a loyalist. British will offer limited amnesty in return for surrender. Negotiations fail.

1779: British defenses at present site of Fort Wadsworth include earthen batteries, redoubt, 26-gun platform, and hot-shot furnace. In the winter, the Kills freeze and soldiers are able to march across.

1783: Evacuation Day, the British leave NYC. Loyalists

forfeit their property, but are given grants in Nova Scotia by the British. Many Hessians decide to stay. Staten Island is deforested.

1799:   Quarantine Station established at Tompkinsville.

1800   Population of Staten Island is 4,564.

1807:   Embargo Act prohibits American ships from leaving US ports for foreign destinations. Maritime trade in New York harbor crippled.

1812:   War declared against Britain. British ships blockade Atlantic ports. State and federal governments authorize telegraph observatories on Staten Island and signal poles in case the British invade by sea. Enemy ships are sighted off Sandy Hook in NJ, but do not enter the Narrows. Daniel D. Tompkins, governor of New York State, oversees establishment of Fort Tompkins at the top of the hill above Fort Richmond (presently Fort Wadsworth).

1816:   The Richmond Turnpike Company builds a road (presently Victory Blvd) from Tompkinsville to Travis, facilitating travel between New York and Philadelphia. The company, owned by Daniel D. Tompkins, also receives authorization to operate a ferry between Staten Island and Manhattan.

1817:   First steam ferry between Staten Island and Manhattan.

1827:   July 4, New York State abolishes slavery.

1828:   Captain John Jackson, first recorded black landowner on Staten Island, buys land near present-day Charleston.

1830s: Newly emancipated blacks from Manhattan move to the Sandy Ground area around Travis, Charleston, and Woodrow. Free black oystermen from Maryland begin to settle there also.

1833:   Sailors' Snug Harbor admits first residents.

1835:   New Brighton is developed as a suburban community.

1836–43: William H. Vanderbilt buys land where Miller Field now stands.

1837:   The Island's first newspaper published, the *Richmond County Mirror*.

1843–44: Henry David Thoreau tutors the sons of William Emerson; Thoreau describes the Island's beauties in letters home.

1850:   Antonio Meucci arrives, hoping to patent his inventions.

1851:   St. Joseph's Church in Rossville, the borough's oldest extant Catholic church building, is built. Giuseppe Garibaldi comes to live with Meucci, and works as a candle maker.

1856:   A wooden lighthouse is built on the site of Miller Field; called the Elm Tree Light, it replaces an actual elm tree used as a navigational aid. The Staten Island Historical Society is formed.

1858:   Men from Tompkinsville, Clifton, and nearby neighborhoods, fearful of yellow fever, burn down the Quarantine station, destroying all the hospital buildings after moving the patients outdoors.

1860:   Telegraph comes to Staten Island. Passenger trains run between Eltingville and Clifton.

1861:   By the beginning of the Civil War, Fort Wadsworth (then called Fort Richmond) is complete and ready to defend the harbor.

1863:   In August, the draft is set in motion; Staten Island has 2,200 eligible men; 594 names are drawn and these men are notified to appear before the provost marshal at Jamaica. Most take advantage of a clause allowing them to pay the supervisors $300 to get off, or else they find substitutes. About 150 simply don't report. A second call comes in October. During this period, six army camps are established on the North and East Shores. A shot tower is built along the East Shore to supply ammunition. Draft Riots spread from Manhattan to Staten Island; violence continues for six days as houses owned by blacks are burned; blacks are hunted down, beaten, and at least five are killed. New Brighton town minutes report that people throw potato peelings, pea shells, and so on into the streets to be eaten by swine.

1864:   In March and August, the federal government issues more calls for soldiers. Supervisors offer $200 per man and a like amount to the "broker who procured him." Or, to avoid service, men can pay $600 to county supervisors, a sum soon raised to $700.

1865: In February, 446 men are summoned by name to be drafted, but they still find substitutes. The Civil War ends. Gas street lighting comes to Staten Island.

1866: New Brighton, Edgewater, and Port Richmond are incorporated as villages.

1867: Anna Leonowens, famous for having taught the children of the King of Siam, opens a school in West Brighton on Richmond Terrace.

1870s Ethnic enclaves develop: the French in Grant City, Italians in Rosebank, Poles in Linoleumville, Germans in Stapleton, Scandinavians in Port Richmond.

1870: Swinburne Island is created as the site for the Quarantine hospital. First defense of America's Cup off Staten Island. New York Yacht Club clubhouse is next to Alice Austen House in Rosebank.

1871: The boiler of the ferry *Westfield II* explodes at South Ferry in Manhattan, killing 66 on the spot and injuring 200 more, 60 of whom die of their injuries.

1872: Entrepreneur George Law buys up land in what is now St. George. Eventually the town will be named for him.

1873: Hoffman Island is finished as part of the Quarantine. Quarantine Station at Rosebank built with the understanding that there would be no detention hospital on the site.

1874:   Mary Ewing Outerbridge introduces lawn tennis to the US from Bermuda.

1880:   The nation's first lawn tennis tournament is played in New Brighton.

1881:   The S.S. White Dental Works opens a factory at Seguine Point in Prince's Bay, becoming a major Staten Island employer. The Natural Science Association is formed; it will develop into the Staten Island Institute of Arts and Sciences.

1883:   Father John Drumgoole founds St. Vincent's Home for Homeless Newsboys at Mount Loretto, having already started such a refuge in Lower Manhattan.

1884:   First Jewish congregation established in Tompkinsville, Congregation B'nai Jeshurun.

1889:   Staten Island is linked to New Jersey by a railroad bridge.

1896:   Population of Staten Island climbs above 60,000.

1898:   Staten Island becomes part of NYC; voters approve the referendum with a 73 percent margin.

1905:   New York City takes over the operation of the Staten Island Ferry.

1906:   Borough Hall is dedicated in St. George.

1907:   Procter & Gamble opens a factory in Mariners Harbor, which will be renamed Port Ivory.

1912:   Staten Island Range Light is lit for the first time to guide ships into the Lower Bay.

1913:   Sea View Hospital for tuberculosis opens.

1916:   Violent protests by locals as city builds garbage

disposal plant on an island in Fresh Kills. NYC Health Department closes Staten Island waters to oyster fishing because of typhoid.

1917:   Staten Island begins using water from NYC's Catskill system.

1918:   *Staten Island Advance* begins publishing a daily newspaper.

1919:   Courthouse at Richmond Town holds final session, moves into present building in St. George. US government converts William H. Vanderbilt farm into coastal air defense station.

1922:   Poet Langston Hughes summers on a Greek-owned truck farm growing produce.

1923:   Shafts dug on Staten Island and in Brooklyn for a subway line to run under the Narrows. The project never comes to fruition.

1924:   Typhoid epidemic leads NYC Health Commissioner to close all oyster beds in NY Harbor. US Gypsum buys existing plaster mills in New Brighton and moves in, becoming a major Staten Island employer.

1926:   The first commercial airport opens in New Springville.

1928:   The Goethals Bridge and Outerbridge Crossing open, joining Staten Island to NJ. Admiral Byrd tests his new plane, a Ford Trimotor, at Miller Field; he will use it on his first trip to Antarctica.

1930:   Population is 158,346.

1931:   Bayonne Bridge opens.

1934:   Staten Island trolley lines are replaced with bus service.

1936:   Staten Island Zoo opens.

1937:   Nation's first free trade port opens in Stapleton. Heavy rains flood Jersey St in New Brighton, causing a tenement to collapse; 19 people are killed. The FDR Boardwalk in South Beach is dedicated, followed by eight hours of entertainment including fireworks and a beauty contest.

1938:   Great Kills is selected for landfill.

1940:   Population is 174,441.

1942:   Cargo ships depart from Staten Island Terminal at Stapleton for World War II battlefields.

1941–45: During World War II, seacoast guns and observation towers are constructed at Miller Field. Italian prisoners of war are housed at Fort Wadsworth.

1946:   Fire destroys the St. George Ferry Terminal, killing three and injuring 280.

1947:   A near-record 26 inches of snow fall on Staten Island on Dec 26–27. Halloran Hospital, formerly used by US Army, becomes Willowbrook State Hospital. Jacques Marchais Tibetan Museum opens.

1948:   A drive-in movie theater opens at New Springville, adjoining the airfield. Fresh Kills Landfill opens "temporarily."

1950:   Alice Austen goes to Farm Colony. Population is 191,555.

1951:   Bobby Thomson, a native Staten Islander, defeats the Brooklyn Dodgers with the historic home run known as "the shot heard round the world."

1952:   Richmondtown Restoration (now Historic Richmond Town) opens.

1956:   Staten Island Community College opens in St. George as part of City University of New York.

1959:   Construction of Verrazano-Narrows Bridge begins as buildings near Fort Wadsworth are demolished along the bridge approaches.

1960:   Population is 221,991. TWA Lockheed Super Constellation and United Airlines DC-8 collide in the air; the TWA wreckage plummets to Miller Field. Bethlehem Steel Corp, among Island's largest employers for years, closes its ship-building plant on Richmond Terrace, though its propeller plant and foundry will continue to operate for another eleven years. Hurricane Donna raises a storm surge of 11 feet in New York harbor.

1963:   Piels Brothers Inc., Staten Island's last remaining brewery, closes. Brush fires destroy more than 100 houses in three communities, including many homes in Sandy Ground.

1964:   The Verrazano-Narrows Bridge opens; it will change the face of Staten Island.

1969:   Miller Field, with the last grass runway in New York City, is deactivated.

1970:   Population is 295,443.

1971:   Quarantine station in Rosebank closes after almost a century of service. Notre Dame College on Grymes Hill closes; St. John's University takes over the campus. *Staten Island Advance* reporter Jane Kurtin investigates conditions at Willowbrook State School; Geraldo Rivera follows with TV exposé leading to eventual closing of the facility.

1972:   Miller Field becomes part of the National Park Service's Gateway National Recreation Area. Fort Wadsworth included in legislation as future recreation area, but remains under military administration.

1973:   Staten Island Mall opens. City buys land at Sailors' Snug Harbor for a cultural center.

1975:   New York City fiscal crisis cuts ferry service between 11pm and 5am for a month. Fare raised from 5 to 25 cents.

1976:   Last of retired seamen leave Sailors' Snug Harbor for North Carolina. Snug Harbor Cultural Center is established.

1980:   Population is 352,029. Sandy Ground Historical Society is formed.

1985:   First mosque opens.

1986:   Brooklyn landfill closes, its daily load of 22,000 tons of garbage adding to the burden of Fresh Kills landfill. One-way toll on Verrazano-Narrow Bridge begins.

1989:   NYC Board of Estimate eliminated by Supreme

Court decision, giving Staten Island less power in City government. NY State Legislature passes a bill authorizing a study on SI secession. State orders Fresh Kills landfill closed by July 1991.

1990: Population is 278,977. Fare on Staten Island Ferry doubled to an all-time high of fifty cents.

1991: After 84 years, Procter & Gamble closes its Staten Island factory.

1993: Staten Islanders in a non-binding referendum vote to secede from NYC by a margin of almost 2 to 1. In the same vote, Staten Islanders vote for mayoral candidate Rudolph Giuliani, who works behind the scene to defuse secession sentiment.

1995: Battery Weed at Fort Wadsworth taken over by the Park Service.

1996: State Court of Appeals disallows secession unless the City of New York requests it, unlikely since the City would lose one-fifth of its territory and some 375,000 people. The New York State Senate agrees to close the Fresh Kills Landfill. In blizzard conditions, 30 inches of snow fall on Staten Island.

1997: Ferry fare abolished.

1999: Staten Island Yankees play their first home game, at the College of Staten Island.

2000 Population 443,728.

2001: March 22, the last of an estimated two billion tons of garbage is barged to the Fresh Kills Dump. (The dump will re-open briefly to accept material from the World Trade Center.) September 11, terrorist attack on the World Trade Center: over 270 Staten Islanders die, including police officers, fire fighters, and office workers.

2003:   Power failure darkens New York City, seven other states, and parts of Canada, for at least 12 hours, the largest blackout to affect the region since 1965. The *Andrew J. Barberi* ferry hits a concrete maintenance pier in St. George, killing 11 passengers and injuring 70. The ship's pilot is sentenced to 18 months in prison.

2010:   Work begins upgrading the Staten Island Expressway, the first time since it opened. The *Andrew J. Barberi* slams into a dock at the St. George again; this time the cause is mechanical failure.

2011:   August 27, residents of low-lying areas are ordered to evacuate as tropical storm Irene threatens New York City. The City escapes catastrophic damage, though areas of Staten Island are flooded. Staten Island celebrates its 350th anniversary.

2012:   November 29, Hurricane Sandy devastates Staten Island. Twenty-three people die, more than half the total in NYC. Others are saved by heroic rescues from helicopters or boats; houses are swept off their foundations, roads inundated. Grief and recriminations follow, but the storm's destruction makes New York aware of its precarious position and the implications of past decisions.

INDEX

NB: In cases where multiple references of equivalent length are given, the main or most explanatory reference (if there is one) is shown in bold.

9/11 Memorial 25

9/11 "people's memorial" 40

Abbott, Mabel 99

Abolitionists on Staten Island 30, 167–68

Abraham J. Wood House 49

Adams, John 163, 164, 165

African American communities 34, 75, 78ff, 176–77, 179

African Methodist Episcopal Zion Church (*see A.M.E. Zion*)

Akerly, Dr. Samuel 107

Almirall, Raymond F. (1869–1939) 204

Ambrose Channel 90, 92

American Magazine 91

American Society of Civil Engineers 152

A.M.E. Zion Church 80, 81–82, 83, 84

Ammann, Othmar H. (1879–1965) **151**, 152, 153, 155

Anastasia, Albert 197

Andrew J. Barberi, ferry 60, 246

Andros, Sir Edmund 234

Angels' Circle 40

Arthur Kill **19**, 37, 74, 76, 117, 119, 148, 149, 164, 206

Arthur Kill Lift Bridge 148–49

Arthur Kill Salvage Yard 38

Asians on Staten Island 36, 37

Atlantic Salt 29

Austen, Alice 126–134, 201, 209, 242; (grave of) 43

Ballou's Pictorial Drawing-Room Companion 76

Baltimore & Ohio Railroad 149, 153

Barnes, William 66

Battery Duane 170

Battery Weed 169, 170, 171–72, 173, 245

Bayles, Richard M. 168

Bayley-Seton Hospital 34

Bayley, Dr. Richard 35, 48, 140

Bayonne Bridge 151–52, 242

Beil, Carlton B. 211

Bethlehem Steel 33, 149, 243

Billopp, Christopher **162**, 164, 165, 235

Bilotti, Tommy 188; (grave of) 43

Black communities on Staten Island (*see African American*)

Bloomberg, Michael 8

Bluebelt program 24, 47, **147**

Borough Hall 26, 27

Botanical Garden 61, **219**

Boy Scouts 112

Breweries 34, 41, 243

Bridges:
   Arthur Kill Lift 148–49
   Bayonne 151–52, 242
   Goethals **150**, 241
   Outerbridge Crossing **150**, 241
   Verrazano-Narrows 112, 152–55, 215, 244

Brinley, C. Coapes 133

British (early settlers) 159, 176; (in Revolutionary War) 48, 111, 162ff, 235

Britton, Elizabeth 97

Britton, Nathaniel Lord 96; (house of) 47

Bronston, Dr. William 207

Brood 2, cicadas 101, 102

Bulls Head 36, 177

Burdge, Ed 91

Burial grounds, Native American 160

Burke, George 50

Burr, Aaron 31

Byrd, Admiral 241

Cameron, Sir Roderick 39

Camp High Rock 111–14

"Captain's Row" 31

Caro, Robert 12

Carrère and Hastings 26

Carrère, John M., grave of 43

Cass, William and Catherine 93

Castellano, Paul 187, 188; (grave of) 43

Cemetery of the Resurrection 140

Charles II, King 176, 234

Charleston 52

Chesapeake Bay 76, 77, 79, 171

Cicadas **101**, 102, 103, 220

Civil War 170, 171, 181, 167–69, 238

Clay Pit Ponds State Park 52

Clifton **34**, 109, 143

Coblentz, Edna (see Marchais, Jacques)

Cocclestown (see Richmondtown)

College of Staten Island 208, 243

Conference House 163–66, 209–10

Coppola, Francis Ford 189

Corner, James 120, 121

"Crimson Beech" 92–93

Crooke, John J. 48

Cropsey, Jasper Francis, grave of 43

Cunard family 129

Cunard, Sir Edward 44

Curtis, George William **30**, 94, 95, 168; (grave of) 43

Davis, Charles Vincent (1912–67) 27, 28

Davis, Thomas E. 29

Davis, William T. 14, 44, 46, 59, 98, 99–102; (grave of) 43

Day, Dorothy 140

Decker, Isaac 162

Denino, Carlo 216

Denton, Daniel 94

De Vries, David Pietersen 156, 157, 232, 233

Dongan Hills 44

Dongan, Thomas 23, 42, 44, 234; (site of mansion of) 31

Donjon Marine Company 38

Dreiser, Theodore 67

Drisius, Rev. Samuel 234

Drumgoole, Fr. John 51, 52, 240

Dutch, early colonists 18, 75, 117, 156, 157, 158, 176, 231–34; (burial customs of) 42

Dutch West India Company 156

East Shore 39ff, 238

Eisenstaedt, Alfred 133

Elm Tree Lighthouse 89, 237

Eltingville 238

Emerson Hill 44

Emerson, Ralph Waldo 103

Emerson, William 44, 103, 104–05

Emerson, Willie 104

Endicott, William C. 172

English 234 (*see also British*)

Esposito, Joe 92, 173

Faber, Eberhard, grave of 43

Falco, Michael 26, **57**, 230

Farm Colony (*see New York Farm Colony*)

Ferry (*see Staten Island Ferry*)

Flagg, Ernest 17, **45**, **50**, 112, 180

Fort Hill Park 163

Fort Knyphausen 163

Fort Richmond (*see Battery Weed*)

Fort Tompkins 169, 170, 171, 172, 173

Fort Wadsworth 94, 157, 163, **169–73**, 210–11, 235, 238, 242, 244

Fort Wadsworth Lighthouse 173

Franklin, Benjamin 164, 165

Fresh Kills 37, 158, 160

Fresh Kills, landfill site 116–20, 241, 244, 245

Freshkills Park 120–25, 212

Gambino crime family 187, 197

Gangsters on Staten Island 187–89

Garbage disposal 122 (*see also Fresh Kills*)

Garcia, Alvaro, grave of 43

Garibaldi-Meucci Museum 183, 215

Garibaldi, Giuseppe 179, 180, 181, **182**, 215, 237

Gateway National Recreation Area **22**, 49, 173, 244

Gay, Sidney Howard 168

George III, King 162

Germans on Staten Island 34, 177, 179, 239

Morris, Ira K. 160, 177, 200

Moses, Robert 8, 11–13, 21, 37, 46; (and Fresh Kills) 117, 118, 119; (and Richmond Parkway) 113, 114, 115, 116; (and Verrazano-Narrows Bridge) 153, 154, 155

Moses' Mountain 116, 213

Mosley, Lois A.H. 82, 83–84

Moulton, Gretta 113

Mount Loretto Unique Area 51

Munn, Edward Stopford 127

Nance, Native American 160

Nation, Carrie 71

Native Americans 57, 99, 117, 159; (burial grounds and customs) 42, 160; (see also Lenape)

New Brighton 29, 237, 238, 239, 240, 241, 242

New Dorp 39, 41, 179

New Dorp Gardens, Inc. 113, 114

New Dorp Lighthouse 89, 90

Newhouse Center for Contemporary Art 218

New Jersey, border and border disputes 19, 148

New Netherland 18, 156, 157, 231, 232

New Springville 177, 241

New York City Farm Colony 133, 194–201, 242

New York Daily Tribune 107

New York Times 152, 205

Nicolls, Richard 19

Noble, John A. 38, 70–74, 219; (photograph of) 57

Noble, John "Wichita Bill" 70–71, 72, 73

Noble Maritime Collection 73, 89, 219

North Shore 24ff, 163, 167, 184, 238

Northfield, ferry 59, 60

Old Dorp (Oude Dorp) 40, 158, 234

Old Orchard Shoal Light 85

Olmsted, Frederick Law 50, 58, 81, 96, 105–10, 115, 121, 145, 146, 175, 211

Olmsted-Beil House 211

Orbach, Nathan 112

Order Sons of Italy in America 183

Girl Scouts 111, 112, 113

Giuliani, Rudolph 245

Godfather, The; "Godfather House" 189

Goethals Bridge 150, 241

Gotti, John 187

Grant City 239

Grasmere 39

Gratacap, Louis Pope 97

Great Kills 48, 74, 158, 242

Greeks on Staten Island 177–78, 241

Green, Bradford 115

Greenbelt 102, 110ff, 212–14

Grymes Hill 44, 103, 180, 244

Grymes, Suzette 44

Guidos 189–90

Hagenhofer, Robert 114

Hand, Phebe 142

Hannah, Native American 159

Heade, Martin Johnson 117

Hessian troops 111, 164, 236

High Rock Park 111–16, 212

Historic Richmond Town 45, 46, 163, 176, 198, 214–15, 243

Hoffman Island 21, 128, 194, 239

Hollick, Charles Arthur 97

Hollick, Dr. Frederick 193

Hormann, August, grave of 43

Horn, Axel 28

Hotels 222

Howe, Admiral Richard 164, 165

Howe, Gen. William 162, 163, 164, 165

Howland Hook 33

Hudson River 19

Hudson, Henry 8, 54, 94, 156, 170, 231

Hughes, Langston 36, 241

Huguenots 158, 176, 235

Huguenots, Memorial Church of 50

Hunt, Richard Morris 145

Hunter, George H. 82–83, 84

Hurricane Sandy 39–40, 85, 175, 178, 246

Hylan, John 153

Irish on Staten Island 177, 179, 184

Isle of Meadows 20

Italian Historical Society of America 155

Italians on Staten Island 10, 34, 36, 37, 39, 40, 177, 179ff, 239

Jackson, John 79, 236

Jacques Marchais Gallery 137

Jacques Marchais Museum of Tibetan Art **134**, 217, 242

Jensen, Oliver 133

Jersey Shore, TV show 8, 190

Jewish communities on Staten Island 37, 177, 179, 240

John Cardinal O'Connor Lighthouse 51

John H. and Elizabeth J. Elsworth House 49

Johns, H.W., mining company 17

Johnson, President Lyndon B. 154

Joseph H. Seguine House 49

Katherine Walker, ship 86

Kennedy, Robert 207

Kieft, Willem 157, 232, 233

Kill van Kull **18**, 74, 148, 152, 158

Klauber, Harry 137, 139

Koch, Robert 202, 203

Korean Veterans Highway 116

Kreischer, Balthazar 52

Kurlansky, Mark 74

Kurtin, Jane 244

La Guardia, Fiorello 11, 21, 118

Lafever, Minard 65

Landfill (*see Fresh Kills*)

Law, George 239

Lemon Creek Park 49

Lenape, Native Americans 57, 74, 75, 156, **158–59**, 220, 231–34; (burial grounds of) 160

Leng, Charles W. 14, 44, 59, 100; (grave of) 43

Leonowens, Anna 239

Life magazine 133, 139

Lighthouse Depot 86

Lighthouse Hill 45

Lighthouses, general 85ff
  Elm Tree **89**, 237
  Fort Wadsworth 173

New Dorp 89, **90**

Old Orchard Shoal 85

Prince's Bay (John Cardinal O'Connor) 51

Range lights 89

Robbins Reef 86–89

Staten Island Range 45, **92**, 240

Swash Channel Range Rear 90

West Bank 90

Lind, Jenny 167

Lindenthal, Gustav 152

Linoleumville 239

Lipton, Barbara 137

Livingston, William 166

Lovelace, Richard 234

MacKenzie, Rev. Aeneas 47

Mafia on Staten Island 187, 188, 197

Magicicada (*see Cicadas*)

Mandia, Grace 132

Mandolin Brothers 31, **32**

Manee, Abraham 50

Marchais, Jacques 134, 135–39

Marine Society 35, 62, 65, 68

Mariners Harbor **31**, 240

Maryland 79, 237

Mauch Chunk, steam

May, Cornelis 232

McCartney, Paul 32

McMillen, Loring 46

Melville, Herman 69

Melville, Thomas 67 (grave of) 43

Melyn, Cornelis 27, 233

Meteor, cruising yacht

Metro, free newspaper

Meucci, Antonio 180, 182, 215, 237

Mexicans on Staten Isl 36, 179

Midland Beach 39, **41**, 179

Midline 44ff

Miller Field 41, 89, 143 **174**, 237, 241, 242, 2 244

Miller, James Ely 174

Mitchell, Joni 32

Mitchell, Joseph 82

Mob Wives, TV show 8, 1

Moby-Dick 143

Montgomery, Brookings 1

Moravian Cemetery 69, 41–43, 144, 213

Oude Dorp (*see Old Dorp*)

Our Lady of Mount Carmel shrine 184–86, 216

Outerbridge Crossing **150**, 241

Outerbridge, Eugenius Harvey 150–51

Outerbridge, Mary 151, 240

Oystering, oysters 49, 74ff, 84, 214, 237, 241

Palma, Joseph 22

Pauw, Michael 156, 232

Pavilion Hotel 29, 167

Peach War 157, 233

Pellegrino, Wendy 40

Penn, William 160

Periaugers 57

Phipps, Mrs. Howard 112

Piels brewery 34, 243

Pig War 156, 232

Planters Hotel 167

Pleasant Plains 51

Poles on Staten Island 36, 179, 239

Poorhouse (*see New York Farm Colony*)

Port Ivory (*see Howland Hook, Mariners Harbor*)

Port of New York Authority 150, 151, 152

Port Richmond **31**, 33, 142, 143, 178, 179, 239

Postcards, 9/11 memorial 25

Pouch, William T. 112

Prall's Island 20

Primiano, Joseph 138

Prince's Bay **49**, 74, 75, 76, 158

Prince's Bay Lighthouse 51

Procter & Gamble 33, 149, 240, 245

Quarantine facility 21, 128, 192–94, 237, 239, 244

Ralph's Famous Italian Ices 216

Randall, Robert Richard 62, 63–64, 217

Randall, Thomas 62–63

Range lights 89

Raritan Bay 74, 85, 107

Regrenier, Paulus 50

Restaurants 222–25

Revolutionary War 48, 111, 162ff, 235

Richmond (*see Historic Richmond Town*)

Richmond County Courthouse 26, 27

Richmond County Mirror 59, 237

Richmond, Duke of 176, 234

Richmond Parkway 114–16 114

Richmond Terrace **28**, 61, 163, 167, 177, 235, 239

Richmondtown (*see Historic Richmond Town*)

Rivera, Geraldo 207, 244

Robbins Reef 86, 87

Robbins Reef Lighthouse 86–89

Robitzek, Dr. Edward 205

Rockefeller, Nelson 155

Roosevelt, Alice 21

Rosebank **36**, 184, 185, 239, 244

Ross, William E. 37

Rossville 37, 237

Russo, Vito 186

Rutledge, Edward 164, 165

Sailors' Snug Harbor (*see Snug Harbor Cultural Center*)

St. Andrew, Church of 47, 140

St. George **26–28**, 86, 163, 239

St. Joachim and St. Anne, church of 52

St. Joseph's Church 237

St. Mark's Church in-the-Bowery 144

Sam, Native American 159, 160

Sandy Ground 37, 75, 78ff, 237, 243, 244

Scandinavians on Staten Island 177, 239

Schatz, Albert 204

Schmul Park 124

Schuster, Arnold 196, 197

Scorsese, Martin 43

Seaman's Retreat 34–35

Seaview Hospital 201–05, 240

Seguine, Anna 176

Seguine, Joseph H. 50

Seguine Point 192, 240

Selikoff, Dr. Irving 205

September 11 (*see World Trade Center; 9/11*)

Serpentinite 16–17, 51

Seton, St. Elizabeth Ann 35, **140**

Seventeen-year locusts (*see Cicadas*)

Shaw, Francis George 168

Shaw, Robert Gould 31; (cenotaph of) 43, 167

Shepherd, Barnett 65, 80, 82

Sheridan, General Philip 171

Ships' graveyard, Arthur Kill 38

Shooter's Island 20–21

Shrine of Our Lady of Mt Carmel 184, 216

Silvestro, Ralph 216

Skinner, Alanson Buck 98

Slavery, slaves 79, 176–77

Snug Harbor Cultural Center 30, 61ff, 217–19, 244

Sono, Masayuki 25

South Beach 39, **40**, 143, 158, 242

"South Pole" 210

South Shore 48ff

Southern planters on Staten Island 29, 167

Sri Lankans on Staten Island 34, 179

Stahr, Frederick Charles (1876–1946) 27

Stapleton **34**, 142, 239, 242

Staten Island Advance 9, 39, 241

Staten Island Agricultural Society 108

Staten Island Ballet 205

Staten Island Botanical Garden 61, **219**

Staten Island Ferry 54ff, 236, 240, 245

Staten Island Gazette and Sentinel 69

Staten Island Historical Society 100, 129, 132, 133, 237

Staten Island Institute of Arts & Sciences 95, 100

Staten Island Museum 219

Staten Island Range Light 45, **92**, 240

Staten Island Standard 200

"Staten Italy" 187–90

Steinman, David 153

Stephen D. Barnes House 31

Stewart, A.T. 144

Stiles, T.J. 58

Stuyvesant, Peter 158, 234

Sutton, Willie 195–97 195

Swan Hotel 177

Swash Channel Range Rear Lighthouse 90

Swinburne Island **21**, 128, 194, 239

Tate, Gertrude 129, **130**, 131, 132, 133

Taylor, Moses 167

TB (*see Tuberculosis*)

Terminal moraine **15**, 19, 48, 51, 169

Tesschenmaker, Petrus 107, 235

Thoreau, Henry David 44, 96, 103–05, 237

Tibetan art museum (*see Jacques Marchais*)

Tibicen (*see Cicadas*)

Todt Hill 16, **45**, 180, 187

Tompkins, Daniel D. 33, 236

Tompkinsville **33**, 156, 163, 179, 192, 193, 240

Tosomock Farm 108

Totten, Joseph G. 171

Tottenville 53, 75, 81, 158

Townsend & Downey, shipbuilders 21

Transportation 220

Travis 36, 177

Trudeau, Dr. Edward Livingston 203, 204

Tuberculosis 202, 203, 204, 205

Tyler, Julia Gardiner 29

Udall, Stewart 113

Urban, Erin 72

US Coast Guard 86, 89, 91

US Gypsum 29, 149, 241

Vanderbilt family, general 41, 43, 112, 129, 141ff

Vanderbilt, Cornelius (the "Commodore") 35, 43, 57–58, **141**, 142, 143, 174

Vanderbilt, Cornelius Sr. 142

Vanderbilt, George Washington 174

Vanderbilt, George Washington II 108

Van der Bilt, Jacob 141

Vanderbilt, Jacob H. 44, 58

Vanderbilt, John King 143

Vanderbilt Mausoleum 43, 144–47

Vanderbilt, William H. 41, 43, 108, **143**, **144**, 145, **174**, 237; (burial of) 146

Verrazano, Giovanni da 27, 54, 94, 170, 179, **231**
Verrazano-Narrows Bridge 112, 152–55, 215, 244
Victory Diner, the 178
Virginia 29, 79
Voorlezer's House 47
Waddell, John Alexander Low (1854–1938) 149–50
Waksman, Selman A. 204
Walker, John 87
Walker, Katherine 86–89
Walloons 158, 232
War of 1812 171, 236
Ward, Samuel 165
Ward, Violet 129
Ward's Point 160
Washington, George 163
Wassenaer, Nicolaes van 232
Watering Place (*see Tomp-kinsville*)
Watkins, Helen 139
Watson, Thomas Jr. 112
Weed, Brigadier General Stephen 169; (grave of) 43
West Bank Lighthouse 90–91

West Brighton **30**, 184, 239
West Shore 36ff
Westfield II, ferry 58, 181, 239
Whiskey War 157
Wilhelm II, Kaiser 21
Wilkins, Michael 207
William T. Davis Wildlife Refuge **102**, 111, 214
Willowbrook, neighbor-hood 194
Willowbrook, school 206–08, 244
Willowbrook, stream 206
Wiman, Erastus 26
Wisconsin Glacier 14, 51
Witte Marine Equipment Company 38
Witte, John J. 38
Wolley, Rev. Charles 159
World Trade Center attack 25, 120, 123, 246
World War II 21, 33, 173, 174ff, 206, 242
Worthington, Charles 153
Wright, Frank Lloyd 92–93

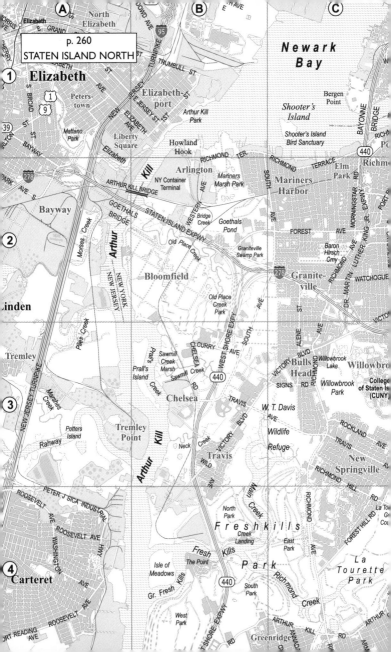

A | **B** | **C**

North Elizabeth

Elizabeth

NORTH AVE

95

TRUMBULL ST

Newark Bay

1 Elizabeth

Peterstown

1
9

39

Mattano Park

Liberty Square

Elizabethport

Arthur Kill Park

Howland Hook

Shooter's Island

Bergen Point

Shooter's Island Bird Sanctuary

BAYONNE BRIDGE

440

Richm

RICHMOND TERRACE

Elm Park

Richm

Po

2 Bayway

278

Arthur Kill

GOETHALS BRIDGE

STATEN ISLAND EXPWY

ARTHUR KILL BRIDGE

Arlington

NY Container Terminal

WESTERN AVE

RICHMOND

Mariners Marsh Park

SOUTH AVE

Mariners Harbor

FOREST AVE

MORNINGSTAR RD

PORT R

DR. MARTIN LUTHER KING JR. EXPWY

Bridge Creek

Goethals Pond

Graniteville Swamp Park

Baron Hirsch Cmy

WATCHOGUE

NEW YORK NEW JERSEY

Bloomfield

Old Place Creek

278

Granite-ville

ST

VICTORY

3 Linden

Pralls Creek

Morses Creek

Old Place Creek Park

CURRY

CHELSEA

WEST SHORE EXPWY

SOUTH AVE

ALENE BLVD

Bulls Head

VICTORY BLVD

RICHMOND AVE

Willowbrook Lake

Willowbro

Willowbrook Park

College of Staten Is (CUNY)

Tremley

Sawmill Creek Marsh

Pralls Island

Sawmill Creek

Chelsea

440

RD

SIGNS

RD

W. T. Davis

TRAVIS

ROCKLAND AVE

Marshes Creek

NEW JERSEY TURNPIKE

Tremley Point

Arthur Kill

Neck Creek

VICTORY BLVD

Travis

Wildlife Refuge

RICHMOND HILL RD

TRAVIS AVE

New Springville

Potters Island

Rahway

WILD AVE

Main Creek

North Park

Creek Landing

Freshkills

East Park

FOREST HILL RD

La To G

4 Carteret

PETER J SICA INDUSTRIAL

ROOSEVELT AVE

ROOSEVELT AVE

WASHINGTON AVE

Isle of Meadows

Fresh Kills

The Point

440

Park

South Park

RICHMOND AVE

La Tourette Park

PORT READING AVE

West Park

Gr. Fresh Kills

WEST SHORE EXPWY

Greenridge

ARTHUR KILL RD

ANNAD

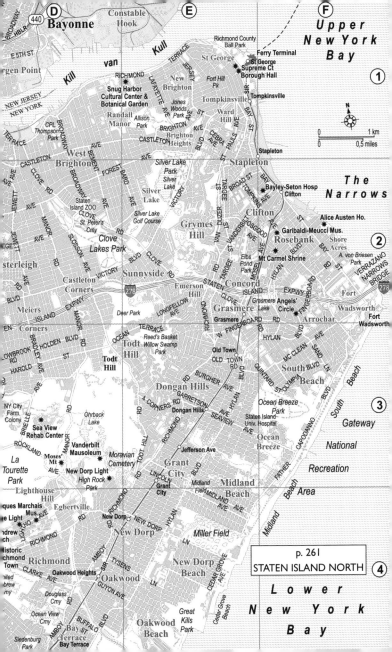

Staten Island North — Map

Grid references (top): D 440 · Bayonne · Constable Hook · E · F

Upper New York Bay

Richmond County Ball Park
Ferry Terminal
St George
Supreme Ct
Borough Hall
①

Kill van Kull

RICHMOND
Snug Harbor Cultural Center & Botanical Garden
New Brighton
Fort Hill Pk
Jones Woods Park
Tompkinsville
Tompkinsville
Ward Hill

NEW JERSEY / NEW YORK

CPL Thompson Park
Randall Manor
Allison Park
Brighton Heights
CASTLETON

West Brighton
Silver Lake Park
Silver Lake
Stapleton
Stapleton

N
0 — 1 km
0 — 0.5 miles

Bayley-Seton Hosp
Clifton

The Narrows

Staten Island ZOO
St. Peter's Cmy
Silver Lake Golf Course
Grymes Hill
Clifton
Rosebank
Alice Austen Ho.
Garibaldi-Meucci Mus.
Shore Acres
A. von Briesen Park
②

Clove Lakes Park
Mt Carmel Shrine
VERRAZANO NARROWS BRIDGE

sterleigh
Castleton Corners
Sunnyside
Emerson Hill
Concord
STATEN ISLAND EXPWY

Meiers Corners
Deer Park
Grasmere Lake
Grasmere
Angels' Circle
Fort Wadsworth
③

Reed's Basket Willow Swamp Park
Todt Hill
Old Town
OLD TOWN
South Beach

Todt Hill
Dongan Hills
Dongan Hills
Ocean Breeze Park
Staten Island Univ. Hospital
Ocean Breeze

NY City Farm Colony
Ohrbach Lake
Sea View Rehab Center
Vanderbilt Mausoleum
Moravian Cemetery
Jefferson Ave
Grant City
Grant City
Midland Field
Midland Beach

South Gateway National Recreation Area
③

La Tourette Park
Moses' Mt
New Dorp Light
High Rock Park
Lighthouse Hill
Egbertville

ques Marchais Mus.
e Light
ndrew
ch
New Dorp
New Dorp
Miller Field

historic Richmond Town
Richmond
Oakwood Heights
Oakwood
New Dorp Beach
p. 261
STATEN ISLAND NORTH ④

Douglass Cmy
Ocean View Cmy
Siedenburg Cmy
Bay St Terrace
Bay Terrace
Oakwood Beach
Great Kills Park

Lower New York Bay

STATEN ISLAND SOUTH
p. 262